PROFILES OF CREATIVE POLITICAL LEADERS

AMERICAN STATESMEN WHO WERE GREAT WRITERS

BY STARR JENKINS

WHITMORE PUBLISHING COMPANY
Ardmore, Pennsylvania

In memory of
Hugh Jerome Jenkins
1929-1953
who would have enjoyed this book.

Contents

Acknowledgments

Many thanks are due to a great teacher, Miss Katherine G. Simons, for planting the seed of American Studies in my mind some twenty years ago. Appreciation is also in order for Dr. Joel M. Jones, Director of American Studies, University of New Mexico, who encouraged this diverse and interdisciplinary project. Thanks, too, must go to Professors William M. Dabney and Ernest Baughman of the University of New Mexico, for supervising the project, reading the manuscript, catching many errors and offering many suggestions for improvement. And special thanks are due also to Mr. and Mrs. Robert I. Stewart, for the use of their Shell Beach writer's den; to Dr. Mona Rosenman, for the use of her electric, bracket-equipped typewriter; to Mrs. Charlene Clark, for the final, frantic typing; and to my wife, Stella, for putting up with it all.

S.J.

San Luis Obispo, California
April 9, 1974

Introduction

Sentences of perfectly clarified wisdom may be literature no less than stanzas of inspired song, or the intense utterances of impassioned feeling....

The great spirits of the past must command us in the tasks of the future.[1]

Woodrow Wilson
Mere Literature

It is the premise of this study that several of America's significant writers have also been statesmen, and that their political, executive and diplomatic accomplishments have in general eclipsed their abilities as literary men. The aims of this work are to present a brief survey of the writings of seven American statesmen who qualify as substantial writers, and to trace the interrelation of their writing abilities and their successful achievement and exercise of power. Secondary aims are to present interesting samples of their better work and furnish bibliographical information for further reading.

The first requirement of this study was the selection of the writer-statesmen whose work was to be surveyed. Two criteria were established for the selection: (1) To qualify as a statesman-writer, the man should be known primarily as a statesman—a significant political leader or influence in nation-building or statecraft. (Thus, an outstanding writer like Washington Irving should not be included, even though he held a significant diplomatic post in later life.) (2) To qualify as a man of letters, a statesman should have a substantial body of good writing, including at least one monumental, readable book or a number of superlative short pieces. On the basis of these criteria, the following statesmen-writers were selected: Benjamin Franklin, John Adams, Thomas Jefferson, John Quincy Adams, Abraham Lincoln, Theodore Roosevelt and Woodrow Wilson.

The second requirement was reading the better works of each of these men until a sense of the man-as-writer emerged; and the third, writing an essay on each. No attempt at seven definitive studies has been made. Nor has there been an attempt at uniformity of treatment, because each man as a writer was a different kind of producer—and his finished works a different kind of collection. Witness Theodore Roosevelt, with thirty-three books, as compared to Lincoln, with essentially none. In surveying these writers to find their best work in the shortest time, the author has made free use of other editors' anthologies of selections. The essays themselves emerge as a blend of survey, biography, quotation and critical comment. Each essay may stand alone or may be considered part of the larger whole.

The works of writers who become statesmen frequently gain their chief interest, not because of poetic achievements, creativity in fiction, or a belletristic beauty of style, but because of the decisive nature of their subject matter and the writer's strategic location in the swirl of human events. Thus,

Benjamin Franklin's *Autobiography,* John Quincy Adams's *Diary* and Lincoln's "Second Inaugural Address" are classics because of their subject matter *combined with* the writer's literary skill. Such works gain added interest because they reflect the minds of men who became decisive for thousands, perhaps millions, of people. Yet I submit that frequently these men were writers of highly creative imagination (though the imagination was channeled into the creating of more advanced organizational systems for man rather than great works of literary art per se). In writing the works they felt impelled to write (usually in and around the heat of organizational strife which is practical politics), these men frequently revealed their creative imagination, perception and considerable literary skill. But for later readers to consider a work literature, it must have quality of mind, dramatic or prophetic interest, style or subject matter such that it will hold the reader's attention and repay the considerable effort in reading. The tedium of details of politics, theory, religious dogma, economics, and military strategies must be overcome by the *human* drama of the actual historical events, actual experienced struggles and scenes, which have a magic for many readers quite as entrancing as the magic of imaginative fiction.

Franklin, the Adamses, Jefferson, Lincoln, Theodore Roosevelt, Wilson—as chiefly working politicians, these men wrote much to articulate and carry out their leadership efforts. Because of this the later reader may be tempted to dismiss much of their writing simply as self-justifying political rhetoric. But at their best—Roosevelt analyzing the czars and emperors of Europe, or the cowboy's life in the Dakotas; Franklin showing the wretched brutality of slavery; Jefferson enunciating the axioms of freedom; John Quincy Adams describing Napoleon's return to Paris; Wilson exposing the antidemocratic procedures of the United States Congress; Lincoln calling for the healing of the battered Union—these men do what any excellent writers do: articulate life and the shattering, reassembling, ascending struggles of man.

3

One remarkable similarity among these very different men is that each demonstrates the talent of the effective leader to lead in thought and spirit as well as action. The spirit must come out of the man's character and education, if not out of the people themselves. The thought may not always be his own; he may rely on more advanced intellectual advisors or precursors, or on his sense of the pulse of the people in their felt needs. But part of his effectiveness will come from his *ability to express the essential thought* in words which move the people to follow him.

This trait can be illustrated by each of these writers. In Woodrow Wilson's 1896 tribute to Walter Bagehot, "A Literary Politician," he quotes the English constitutionalist while admiring his perception of analysis: "The most influential of constitutional statesmen is the one who most felicitously expresses the creed of the moment."[2] Wilson himself, in his essay *Leaders of Men*, described the ideal leader as "one who lends sight to the blind forces of public thought."[3] When young Douglas MacArthur, Roosevelt's aide in 1906, asked him to what ability he attributed his remarkable hold on the people, he replied: "To put into words what is in their hearts and minds but not their mouths." S. E. Morison, in reporting this, adds, "That was it. Lincoln had the same gift."[4] Benjamin Franklin got his start as a successful printer and politician at twenty-two by pamphleteering better than anyone else in the colonies in favor of a popular issue, paper money—and getting the contract from a grateful legislature.[5] John Adams caught the public eye with his 1765 pamphlet "Dissertation on the Canon and Feudal Law," voicing the new spirit of British America: "Let us dare to read, think, speak and write." Jefferson became effective because of his "happy talent of composition" and his "remarkable ... felicity of expression"[6] evidenced in his "Rights of British America." Thus, as the concept of freedom from institutional tyranny took a quantum leap in America, effective persuaders of men became leaders, the men who sensed what could be done and

4

had the power of the poet to fire the masses. A man's ability to clarify his own thoughts in words, to communicate persuasively with other minds, to stir masses of hearts as well as minds with the importance of the thoughts proposed was, if not central, certainly essential to his becoming a leader in the new nation.

The study of Woodrow Wilson has made me realize that the primary reason these men are worth reading today is not found in their actual thoughts, literary eloquence, or even in their character, as rewarding as all these elements are. It is, beyond those, the biographical interest: What did this man— a man who could write well and who achieved much—think about and say in his best finished expressions? What did the organized formulations of his mind have to do with what he was able to achieve in the broad arenas of the world? In short, the reason all these men will always be fascinating to read is the light their writings throw on that most interesting of questions: What makes a great man great?

Another reason the writings of these men are interesting (aside from the principles of government, justice, morality and social welfare expressed, and the literary art of their imagery and style) is this: that each of these men is also a hero of sorts, a striking example of the power of intellect and education coupled with character and individuality to move and change the world for the better. Each of them, through his brain, his heart, and his pen, helped build the new world-nation that is being born.

As to other results: Aside from the survey information compiled on each man, four unifying themes appear. (1) All of these men are primarily writers on politics and government, practical politicians with a sophisticated sense of the theory as well as the history of power. None venture far into *belles lettres* or what is generally called "creative writing" as such (as if the writing necessary to create better government and society were not the most creative of all). (2) All are centrally concerned with *morality*, individual and collective, and specifically with the comparative morality of various governmental forms, laws, and institutions as they affect the morality of the entire society. (3) All are devoted to restraint of government or other organizational powers, in order to protect and enlarge individual freedom and release man's creative energy, today as well as tomorrow. (4) Each also sees America as a new special kind of nation, a divinely ordered opportunity for *the* great experiment in large-scale self-government, in a rich continent untrammeled by too much repressive baggage from the past. Thus, all seven emerge as strong American nationalists committed to constructive reform and the idea of America leading the world toward a new order based on freedom and responsibility.

Another rediscovery made from this study is that of America's continual, real opportunity and its de facto acceptance and encouragement, over the long run, of diversity. Each of these seven men is a distinctive, attractive and interesting personality as well as a significant writer—yet each is attractive and interesting in a different way. No two more different personalities can be imagined than Abraham Lincoln and Theodore Roosevelt. Yet both stood effectively for roughly the same beliefs; in TR's words, they were both "Hamiltonian in their belief in a strong and efficient National Government and Jeffersonian in their belief in the people as the ultimate authority."[7] John Adams and Thomas Jefferson were poles apart in many respects; yet both were ardent advocates of American independence, separation of powers, republican government, widespread public education, freedom of speech and press, and the destruction of unfair aristocratic privilege. Three of the seven, Franklin, Adams and Lincoln, rose from poverty and obscurity to the heights of fame and influence by their own merits, including their abilities to think, write, speak and organize others. Three—Jefferson, John Quincy Adams, and Theodore Roosevelt—were born to moderate wealth and used their aristocratic starting places to good advantage in order to become leaders and talents such that they *had to be employed* by the republic.

6

Truly each one of these men is a fascinating hero and personality no reader would want to miss. And each is a cogent writer whose skill with words opens his mind almost completely to the reader and offers mental delights that may be repeated over a lifetime. And each, too, inspires in his own way the pursuit and cultivation of man's highest creative self, the free individual who on his own responsibility works effectively to make himself and his society better. Each man had a great, challenging, exciting life because he believed in what Lincoln stated was the core of America's mission, "that in due time the weights should be lifted from the shoulders of all men, and that *all* should have an equal chance."[8]

As such, the lives and writings of these seven men show how any self-propelled, competent man or woman can become a contributor, perhaps even a prime mover, in the domestication of the wild world, and in the taming of its most savage inhabitant, man himself. Each of these writers gives us glimpses of the continuity of man's struggle upward toward world order and world peace. Yet they inspire us, too, with the ultimate individual and moral nature of that struggle and with the unfinished—in fact, the scarcely begun—condition of that struggle and the necessity for all of us "to finish the [great and exciting] work we [all] are in."

Benjamin Franklin
America's First Writer and Philosopher

America has sent us many good things, gold, silver, sugar, tobacco, indigo, etc.; but you are the first philosopher, and indeed the first great man of letters for whom we are beholden to her.[1]

David Hume
Letter to Franklin, May 10, 1762

David Hume was not the only contemporary to recognize Benjamin Franklin as a man of literary talent. As Richard Amacher[2] points out, John Adams, one of Franklin's severest critics in politics and other matters, nevertheless had the critical honesty to write of him:

He had wit at will. He had humor that, when he pleased, was delicate and delightful. He had a satire that was good-natured or caustic, Horace or Juvenal, Swift or

9

Rabelais, at his pleasure. He had talents for irony, allegory, and fable, that he could adapt with great skill to the promotion of moral and political truth. He was master of that infantine simplicity which the French call *naiveté*, which never fails to charm, in Phaedrus and La Fontaine, from the cradle to the grave.[3]

Benjamin Franklin, the fifteenth child in a family of seventeen children, emerged from poverty and obscurity due in part to his ability to write. He was able to succeed in business and make himself a political influence also in part due to his ability to put language effectively on paper. After getting only two years of schooling as a child and reading everything he could get his hands on, he taught himself (at the urging of his father) to write well. He did this by devising an English composition course based on analyzing excellent models of writing (such as Joseph Addison's *The Spectator*). He endeavored to discover their design and technique and to reproduce such design and technique in his own version of similar works.[4] Thus he developed the difficult art of writing simply on complex problems, of arguing persuasively, and of devising plans to solve problems which needed solving. At age sixteen, while still apprenticed to his printer-brother, James, young Ben won a place in his brother's paper, the *New England Courant*, by writing and delivering to the office anonymous editorials that were good enough to win praise from James's editorial circle. Then, at seventeen, Ben took over the editorship of the paper when James was jailed for offending the authorities; and Benjamin continued to publish his own editorials under the name of Silence Dogood.[5] Many of these "Dogood Papers" were serious proposals for the public good made long before he could have profited from them financially or politically. Thus did Benjamin Franklin in 1723 begin to emerge as a leader and thinker because he was first of all a voracious reader and an effective writer.

He soon learned of the added dimension of power given a man who could think and write in a free society. He discovered from firsthand experience the power of a pamphlet to teach an idea or persuade a multitude. At twenty-two, as an aspiring printer in Philadelphia, he wrote a pamphlet using William Petty's ideas to persuade the Pennsylvania Assembly to issue land-secured paper money to relieve the colony's shortage of circulating capital. Franklin's pamphlet, "The Nature and Necessity of a Paper-Currency" (1728), proved to be the best of many pro-paper-money pamphlets of the day.[6] Franklin wrote of it:

It was well received by the common people in general; but the rich men disliked it, for it increased and strengthened the clamour for more money, and they happening to have no writers among them that were able to answer it, their opposition slackened, and the point was carried by a majority in the House. My friends there, who conceived I had been of some service, thought fit to reward me by employing me in printing the money; a very profitable job and a great help to me. This was another advantage gained by my being able to write.[7]

Thus the pamphlet not only persuaded the Assembly to make such an issue but to give Franklin the job of printing it. This not only helped establish him as a successful printer but started him on his astounding career of public service, economic analysis, social organization, cultural and scientific achievement, and political and diplomatic influence.

As printer and editor of the *Pennsylvania Gazette* and as editor and writer of *Poor Richard's Almanac*, he was for twenty-five years a major force for education and entertainment in the American colonies, helping to inculcate thrift and virtue along with common sense, practicality and wit throughout the colonies. He continually reverted to writing to achieve

11

either private or public persuasion, to satirize, to stimulate agriculture, to formulate plans, to articulate political, economic, or scientific theory, or to initiate systems of organization. Anonymous satire, using pseudonyms to heighten the effect (customary in the highly censorial eighteenth century), was one of his favorite modes of expression. He was a prolific letter writer as well, and he even became to his friends in France a writer of humorous literary pieces (the bagatelles) which he ran off on the small press he kept with him outside of Paris for propaganda releases. Without his writing ability (or a trusty Boswell to project his every thought on paper) Franklin would have been a genius emasculated, a da Vinci of diplomacy stillborn.

Franklin's overall works run to ten volumes in Albert Smyth's edition (1905-7), or, as retained in the library of the American Philosophical Society (one of Franklin's many brainchildren), seventy-six volumes containing 13,000 separate documents. These naturally cover almost every subject conceivable to the eighteenth century, and many of course are private letters rather than literary works. The most prominent pieces of his writing still worthwhile for the modern reader divide themselves into several classes: the *Autobiography; Poor Richard's Almanac;* satires; straight reasoned persuasion; the bagatelles (humorous literary trifles to friends); and other writing of historical, political, economic or scientific interest.

The *Autobiography,* though covering only the first fifty-one of Franklin's amazing eighty-four years, is his only book and most fascinating work. It is the great rags-to-riches success story, but one also crowned with the enlargement of the mind of the protagonist so that at age forty-two, instead of merely continuing to amass greater wealth, Franklin retired from business to pursue the scientific, cultural, and public service activities that were more interesting to him. Thereafter he was a free creative spirit, catalyzing constructively and observing sagely in every direction he turned. His list of early offices included public printer for Pennsylvania, clerk of the Assembly, member of the Assembly, postmaster for Philadelphia, postmaster general for the colonies, and colonial agent (essentially ambassador) in England for the colonies of Pennsylvania, Georgia, New Jersey, Rhode Island and Massachusetts. Though a patriotic British colonial, he stood for fairer treatment of, and less trade restriction upon, the American colonies by the mother country. He rightly could foresee America not only as the great nation of the future, but as the great center of a more magnificent and unbeatable British Empire (if the colonies were treated fairly by the homeland) or (if not—reluctantly) as an independent nation free of British control. This may be illustrated by a quote from his letter to Lord Kames of January 3, 1760:

I have long been of opinion, that the *foundations of the future grandeur and stability of the British empire lie in America:* and though, like other foundations, they are low and little seen, they are, nevertheless, broad and strong enough to support the greatest political structure human wisdom ever yet erected. I am therefore by no means for restoring Canada. If we keep it, all the country from the St. Lawrence to the Mississippi will in another century be filled with British people. Britain itself will become vastly more populous, by the immense increase of its commerce; the Atlantic sea will be covered with your trading ships; and your naval power, thence continually increasing, will extend your influence around the whole globe and awe the world![8]

The *Autobiography* was written largely in England in 1771 with later additions made in France in 1784. Unfortunately, since it takes his life only up through 1757, it does not carry through his even more intriguing last thirty-three years. But these years have been well treated in numerous other biographies, and even Franklin's half-complete *Autobiography* is

13

considered a classic in early American literature. His writing is readable, smooth, concise and readily understandable; an air of tolerance, wit and practicality pervades his telling of the interesting story. Though Franklin is obviously proud of his success, he readily admits to his errors and his pride, adding *humility* to his list of strived-for virtues only at the suggestion of a Quaker friend and then admitting that if he ever succeeded with that virtue, he would be "proud of my humility."

Much of the fascination of the book comes from the glimpses it gives of the small colonial cities of the 1720-50 era beginning to grow into the metropolises of today, right during the age of Enlightenment when scientific and industrial developments were gathering force for the revolutionizing of man's technology to come. The time and place were wide open with opportunities, and the way a perceptive young man moved in through ability, hard work, persuasion and social acumen to help remake his society is a great story of the power of the single, self-propelled individual. In the early part of the *Autobiography* Franklin tells with wit not only how he "escaped being a poet, and probably a very bad one" through his father's sound advice, but how "prose-writing had been of great use to me in the course of my life and was a principal means of my advancement." In addition, he was gaining a reputation as a diligent reader and learned young man, so much so that men of affairs, such as Governor Keith of Pennsylvania, Governor Burnet of New York and later Sir Hans Sloane in Britain, sought him out for practical suggestions and serious discussions. It was this kind of upbringing and this success which forever put Ben Franklin on the side of freeing the creativity of the human spirit. Franklin well illustrated his own maxim:

I have always thought that one man of tolerable abilities may work great changes, and accomplish great affairs among mankind, if he first forms a good plan, and, cutting off all amusements or other employments that would divert his attention, makes the execution of that same plan his sole study and business.[9]

One reason the *Autobiography* is such a didactic success story is that Franklin set out carefully to make it so. Discussing the fact that his *Autobiography* was being written a bit at a time (in a letter to Benjamin Vaughan, October 24, 1788), he said:

To shorten the work, as well as for other reasons, I omit all facts and transactions that may not have a tendency to benefit the young reader by showing him from my example, and my success in emerging from poverty, and acquiring some degree of wealth, power, and reputation, the advantages of certain modes of conduct which I observed, and of avoiding the errors which were prejudicial to me.[10]

Despite the triteness of Franklin's didactic purpose, despite his reputation among the Adamses as a freethinking libertine, his life—whether one looks upon him as a successful Puritan or a benign Deist—forms a great chronicle of the power of the released-yet-disciplined individual.

Poor Richard's Almanac, an annual affair (1732-57), was one of the typical popular culture items of the day to assist farmers (the bulk of the population in the rural colonies) in planting their crops and knowing needed and interesting information. Franklin garnished his almanac with his own essays and sayings, wisdom rifled and rewritten from the maxims, proverbs and platitudes of the world, to stress in homely Americanese the virtues of thrift, honesty, simple living, devotion to duty, self-control and self-cultivation. In short, while privately soft-pedaling the paradoxes of Puritan theology, he embraced and advertised middle-class ethics in everyday life and business.[11]

Countless sayings, supposedly composed by the fictitious editor, Richard Saunders, illustrate Franklin's wit and the civilization's wisdom: "A fool and his money are soon parted." "Little strokes fell great oaks." "He that can compose himself, is wiser than he that composes books." "He's a fool that makes his doctor his heir." "Strange that a man who has wit enough to write a satire, should have folly enough to publish it." "Search others for their virtues, thyself for thy vices." "The most exquisite folly is made of wisdom spun too fine." (See my later analysis of the Gettysburg Address, in chapter 5.) "You may talk too much on the best of subjects." "Genius without education is like silver in the mine."[12]

Research into his sources usually demonstrates how Franklin improved upon the source in the matter of metaphor, humor, brevity and overall punch.[13] The best of twenty-five years of these sayings Franklin collected into his widely reprinted short work, "Father Abraham's Oration: 'The Way to Wealth.'" This essay symbolizes, as the fictional Poor Richard listens incognito to the old man extol his wisdom, the extent to which Franklin had built Poor Richard into a widely influential popular institution (much as Ann Landers has become today). The essay also shows Franklin's typical use of the ancient humor device of two characters, one a fool and one a wise man, for mockery and irony. Poor Richard had become a crackerbarrel philosopher who planted Franklinian views amidst the humor sprinkled throughout the publication. Richard Amacher cites several studies to show that Franklin's works reflect conscious imitation (in ideas, rhetorical devices and style) of numerous English authors: Bunyan, Defoe, Addison and Swift, principally; Pope, Thomson, Young, Milton, Dryden, Rowe and Watts, secondarily; plus several available rhetorics of the day.[14] And William Clary concludes, after a study of Franklin as printer and publisher, that

Franklin's two greatest business successes, the *Almanac* and the *Gazette,* were the result not mainly of Franklin's ability as a printer, though this contributed, but of his ability as a writer.[15]

Satires: Among the best of his satires is the blistering "Rules by Which a Great Empire May be Reduced to a Small One," mock advice to Britain (written in 1773 while Franklin was there as agent for the colonies, and planted in the British press) on how to be sure to drive the colonies toward independence. It consists of twenty rules by which the ministers of the king's government, obviously tired of the complexities of ruling a large empire, may speed the breakup of that large entity and thus achieve their apparent aim, the removal from their control of those troublesome outlying parts. In blasting each grievance—that had *already been* perpetrated on the colonies by English ministries, governors and courts—Franklin skillfully portrays twenty different ways in which the colonies are the innocent victims and the British government the tyrannical oppressor, each paragraph forming a hard-hitting satire in itself. The order of the grievances is from the general to the specific, while it is also from the least offensive to the most offensive. His use of italics at the end of each paragraph reminds the reader of the ostensible, ironic purpose of each of these disastrous policies, and clarifies that the colonies must indeed seek and win their own independence to receive justice. Beneath its humor, this piece is so sweeping, so bitter, and so beyond redemption that it is clearly a pre-Paine, pre-Jefferson Declaration of Independence in satire form. (The twenty rules are not very different from the list of grievances given seriously in the Declaration of Independence.) Yet Franklin keeps it light in appearance through his wit, appealing as he always did to the intelligence of his reader as well as to his common sense and sense of justice. For example:

I. In the first place, gentlemen, you are to consider that a great empire, like a great cake, is most easily diminished at the edges. Turn your attention, therefore, first to your remotest provinces; that, as you get rid of them, the next may follow in order.

II. That the possibility of this separation may always exist, take special care the provinces are never incorporated with the mother country; that they do not enjoy the same common rights, the same privileges in commerce; and that they are governed by *severer* laws, all of *your enacting,* without allowing them any share in the choice of legislators. By carefully making and preserving such distinctions, you will (to keep to my simile of the cake) act like a wise gingerbread baker, who to facilitate a division, cuts his dough half through in those places, where, when baked, he would have it *broken to pieces.*[16]

As his "rules" proceed, they begin hitting harder and harder.

IV. However peaceably your colonies have submitted to your government, shown their affection to your interests, and patiently borne their grievances; you are to suppose them always inclined to revolt, and treat them accordingly. Quarter troops among them, who by their insolence may provoke the rising of mobs, and by their bullets and bayonets *suppress* them. By this means, like the husband who uses his wife ill from *suspicion,* you may in time convert your *suspicions* into *realities.*

V.... If you can find prodigals, who have ruined their fortunes, broken gamesters or stockjobbers, these may do well as *governors;* for they will probably be rapacious, and provoke the people by their extortions....

XIX. Send armies into their country under pretense of protecting the inhabitants; but, instead of garrisoning the forts on their frontiers with those troops, to prevent incursions, demolish those forts, and order the troops into the heart of the country, that the savages may be

18

encouraged to attack the frontiers, and that the troops may be protected by the inhabitants. This will seem to proceed from your ill will or your ignorance, and contribute farther to produce and strengthen an opinion among them, *that you are no longer fit to govern them.*[17]

The intensity of Franklin's satire may be illustrated by his note appended to the title of these "rules," that they were "presented to a late minister, when he entered upon his administration."

Another satire of the same bent and time is "An Edict of the King of Prussia," wherein Frederick the Great purportedly proclaims to Britain—on the basis of ancient Saxon settlements there—that English iron foundries are to be closed, her trade restricted, and her hat-makers to be put out of business; Prussian thieves are also to be transported to England, and any Englishmen who protest are to be returned to Prussia for trial according to Prussian law. Thus Franklin clothed in the same phraseology as Parliament had used on the colonies preposterous Prussian claims which made the British arrogance and error clear. To add a further detachment to it, Franklin framed the pompous edict in a few mystified remarks by a neutral observer in Danzig; these comments solidify the hoax upon the gullible while clarifying the meaning for the perceptive.

These two satires, widely reprinted and influential in England, were perhaps only the best known of a long list of short, anonymous propaganda works he planted in the press over the years. (Crane has noted that while Franklin was colonial agent in England 1765-66 he used some forty pseudonyms in his secret barrage of letters to the editors on behalf of America.)[18] Others were "Exporting of Felons to the Colonies" (1751); "The Speech of Miss Polly Baker" (1747); "The Sale of the Hessians" (1777); and "Supplement to the *Boston Independent Chronicle*" (1782). The latter is a Swiftian attack on the British practice of hiring the Indians to fight against the colonists by presenting a gruesome inventory of eight packages of scalps being delivered to England as proof of service and justification for reward. The packets are mentioned in ascending order of horror, from scalps of soldiers, to those of farmers, old men, women, boys, girls and the unborn. Franklin wrote this intricately detailed nightmare, it is interesting to note, while he was enjoying the good life outside Paris, exchanging bagatelles with his French friends, and getting ready to negotiate the peace settlement of that war.

"The Sale of the Hessians" is an equally ingenious earlier blast at another British wartime practice, the sending of mercenary Hessian troops to fight the colonists-now-Americans, couched in terms of the German noble instructing his field marshal to get more of the troops killed off so his (the noble's) fees will be higher.

> My trip to Italy, which has cost me enormously, makes it desirable that there should be a great mortality among them. You will therefore promise promotion to all who expose themselves; you will exhort them to seek glory in the midst of dangers; you will say to Major Maundorff that I am not at all content with his saving the 345 men who escaped the massacre of Trenton. Through the whole campaign he has not had ten men killed in consequence of his orders.[19]

In short, Franklin had learned well Swift's tricks of mock understatement, assumption of objectivity, meticulous yet horrifying detail—the art of clever dramatic compression through the role assumed and skill in stabbing in a thousand places and twisting the knife each time.

Another clever and hard-hitting satire was "The African's Speech to the Divan of Algiers" (also labeled "The Evils of the Slave Trade"), Franklin's last public act before his death in 1790. On the slavery question, Franklin had come in his last years to be a staunch abolitionist, as illustrated by his agreeing to serve as president of the Pennsylvania Abolitionist Society.[20] "The African's Speech" is an excellent parody of white-supremacy rhetoric and logic which had just been vented in the Congress, echoes of which are familiar to this day. Casting his mock pro-slave-trade tirade back a century into a North African Moslem framework made his satirical blade double-edged, against the greedy slaveholders wishing to prolong their extortionate vested interest, and against a benighted religious outlook which would justify such atrocities in the name of kindness, justice and the salvation of enslaved souls.

Are not Spain, Portugal, France and the Italian states governed by despots, who hold all their subjects in slavery, without exception? Even England treats its sailors as slaves; for they are, whenever the government pleases, seized, and confined in ships of war, condemned not only to work, but to fight, for small wages, or a mere subsistence, not better than our slaves are allowed by us. Is their condition then made worse by their falling into our hands? No; they have only exchanged one slavery for another, and I may say a better; for here they are brought into a land where the sun of Islamism gives forth its light, and shines in full splendor, and they have an opportunity of making themselves acquainted with the true doctrine, and thereby saving their immortal souls. Those who remain at home have not that happiness. Sending the slaves home then would be sending them out of light into darkness.[21]

This verbal blast was signed "Historicus" in the eighteenth century manner. Thus ended a sixty-eight year public career, punctuated from start to finish by satiric and effective letters to the press, many of which make good reading today.

Direct Persuasion: Franklin's straight, reasoned persuasion can be seen in his diplomatic correspondence, in his many pamphlets and editorials, in his political works outside of the satirical, or in almost any of his economic writing (although his later adherence to physiocratic economics is decidedly less reasonable than his own earlier work). "An Apology for Printers" is a great soft-sell defense of freedom of the press, issued before the Zenger case helped further the same cause in America. Franklin's letter to the London *Chronicle*, June 18-20, 1772, is a powerful two-paragraph blast against the slave trade as a ghoulish destroyer of thousands, yea, hundreds of thousands, of human lives. This letter was instigated by British self-satisfaction in the famous Sommerset decision whereby a slave escaping his master in England was declared free.

It is said that some generous humane persons subscribed to the expence of obtaining liberty by law for Sommerset the Negro. It is to be wished that the same humanity may extend itself among numbers; if not to the procuring liberty for those that remain in our colonies, at least to obtain a law for abolishing the African commerce in slaves, and declaring the children of present slaves free after they become of age.

By a late computation made in America, it appears that there are now eight hundred and fifty thousand Negroes in the English islands and colonies; and that the yearly importation is about one hundred thousand, of which number about one third perish by the gaol distemper on the passage, and in the sickness called the seasoning before they are set to labour. The remnant makes up the deficiencies continually occurring among the main body of those unhappy people, through the distempers occasioned by excessive labour, bad nourishment, uncomfortable accommodation, and broken spirits. Can sweetening our tea, etc., with sugar, be a circumstance of such absolute necessity? Can the petty pleasure thence arising to the taste, compensate for so much misery produced among our fellow creatures, and such a constant butchery of the human species by this pestilential detestable traffic in the bodies and souls of men? *Pharisaical Britain!* to pride thyself in setting free a single slave that happens to land on thy coasts, while thy merchants in all thy ports are encouraged by the law to continue a commerce whereby so many *hundreds of thousands* are dragged into a slavery that can scarce be said to end with their lives, since it is entailed on their posterity![22]

Franklin, who has a good claim to being America's earliest significant economist, also clarified the uneconomic nature of slavery among his many interesting "Observations Concerning the Increase of Mankind," written 1751, published 1755.

The negroes brought into the English sugar islands have greatly diminished the whites there; the poor are by this means deprived of employment, while a few families acquire vast estates, which they spend on foreign luxuries, and educating their children in the habit of those luxuries; the same income is needed for the support of one [wealthy man] that might have maintained one hundred [poor men]. The whites who have slaves, not labouring, are enfeebled, and therefore not so generally prolific; the slaves being worked too hard and ill fed, their constitutions are broken, and the deaths among them are more than the births; so that a continual supply is needed from Africa. . . . The northern colonies, having few slaves, increase in whites. Slaves also pejorate the families that use them; the white children become proud, disgusted with labor, and, being educated in idleness, are rendered unfit to get a living by industry.[23]

Throughout this original population essay Franklin presupposes the antimercantilist axiom (one still strong in many parts of the world today) that the labor supply is the strength and wealth of the nation; hence the larger the number of working people, the larger the national prosperity and wealth. Thus anything which added to the number of working people increased the nation's wealth; anything that subtracted from the number of people available for work decreased the nation's wealth. Population, Franklin asserted, has a natural tendency to increase up to and beyond the limits of the food supplies available (Malthus's idea in germ form, fifty years before Malthus wrote—though there is no evidence Malthus knew of Franklin's essay till after his first publication).[24] Trade, frugality, opportunity (new unoccupied lands) add to the nation's people supply by encouraging earlier and more fruitful marriages. Slavery, unemployment, poverty, bad government and insecure people, importation of foreign luxuries, profligate living—all these decrease a people and hence the national wealth.

> Hence the prince that acquires new territory, if he finds it vacant, or removes the natives to give his own people room; the legislator that makes effectual laws for promoting trade, increasing employment, improving land by more or better tillage, providing more food by fisheries; securing property, etc., and the man that invents new trades, arts, or manufactures, or new improvements in husbandry, may be properly called *fathers* of the nation, as they are the cause of the generation of multitudes, by the encouragement they afford to marriage.[25]

Yet America, with its vast lands relative to its small population, was a special case, the study of which would reveal the principles at work. Previously Franklin had pondered the same relationships.

The natural livelihood of the thin inhabitants of a forest country is hunting; that of a greater number, pasturage; that of a middling population, agriculture; and that of the greatest, manufactures, which last must subsist the bulk of the people in a full country, or they must be subsisted by charity, or perish.[26]

In short, the economic system is as much a function of the population as the population is a function of the social-ethical-political-technological milieu producing it. America's land to people ratio in 1750 makes wages high and land cheap—a combination that will continue to draw geometric population increases for a long time to come. And the relative prosperity of the rich American farms will cause large families to be generated. All these forces will cause America to double in population every twenty-five years. (Franklin's prediction was on the low side of the actuality for roughly a century.)

From this optimistic land speculator's view of population growth, Franklin foresaw that British America would surpass the mother country in people in a century. Elsewhere (as in the Kames letter previously referred to) he predicted that the British Empire's great future strength lay in growing in North America (as soon as the French were ousted), even hinting that the capital of Britain would eventually move to the New World to recognize that fact. The way to cement these far-flung future domains to the crown was to have each be a nation in parallel to Britain, all English freedoms secured to its citizens under its own representative government, subject to the king's veto as outlined in Franklin's Albany Plan of Union, 1754. (This plan, which also provided for unification of the colonies into one federation, was turned down by London as too much favoring the colonials, and by the individual assemblies for threatening their cherished local control.) Franklin conceived that this new empire of numerous equally free British nations (the Commonwealth) would form a huge, unbeatable free

British Empire of the future. The relationship of Franklin's ideas to America's businessman's outlook and its philosophy of manifest destiny and world-wide-freedom-through-our-efficiency-and-power should be evident. The fact that for most of our most formative century he was also our most influential writer stresses again the power of his simple sounding pen.

Though a brilliant conversationalist, Franklin relied on writing and private persuasion, rather than oratory, for capturing his thoughts and achieving most of his effectiveness. Yet in his "Proposals Relating to the Education of Youth of Pennsylvania" (which led to the College of Philadelphia, later the University of Pennsylvania), he discusses oratory as a subject worthy of study.

> Modern political oratory being chiefly performed by the pen and press, its advantages over the ancient in some respects are to be shown; as that its effects are more extensive, more lasting, etc.[27]

The whole essay makes a strong case for improving public or private education for greater efficiency and greater benefit to society and the individual. Coming from the self-made printer, understandably it is also not scornful of the mechanical or practical or agricultural skills (and is correspondingly light in emphasis on classical knowledge). Judging from this essay one would assume that Benjamin Franklin would strongly approve the present movement for greater vocational usefulness in higher and secondary education.

Though Franklin did some of his most effective work aiding his province and later the rebelling colonies in war, he was a lifetime advocate of moderation, fairness, negotiation and peace. In spite of his great dreams of empire, his most famous quotation on war has been *"There never was a good war or a bad peace."*[28] After the peace settlement with Britain, he wrote (ten days after his seventy-seventh birthday):

26

At length we are in peace, God be praised, and long, very long, may it continue. All wars are follies, very expensive, and very mischievous ones. When will mankind be convinced of this, and agree to settle their differences by arbitration? Were they to do it, even by the cast of a die, it would be better than by fighting and destroying each other.[29]

How soon will we learn this lesson, both in settling international differences and domestic ones, such as strikes?

Franklin's most literary productions in the *belles lettres* sense are the bagatelles (or trifles), his handful of humorous essay-letters, written to particular women in France while he was enjoying (as a widower in his seventies) his diplomatic and social life outside Paris. He printed these essays, some of which might more properly be called exercises in courtly love, on his personal press, in the village of Passy where he lived, so that he could pass them around in published form to a few friends. One copy of them bound in a volume exists in the Yale Library—from which Robert E. Amacher has reprinted (with much textual and editorial information) *Franklin's Wit and Folly: The Bagatelles,* 1953. "Franklin and the Gout," "The Whistle," "The Ephemera," and the "The Elysian Fields" are classics worthy of any American literature anthology. All are brief, complete and artful, and radiate wit, charm and thoughtfulness. They reveal Franklin the artist as well as Franklin the humorist. In the mock dialog, "Franklin and the Gout," Ben Franklin, one of the many geniuses who have suffered from the sore-toe disease, skillfully satirizes himself while presenting his theories on the connection between degenerative ailments and the lack of exercise. Madame Gout as she speaks serves as Franklin's conscience, giving him stabs of excruciating pain for his various sins against his own health (plus other sins of laziness, gluttony, injustice, self-deception, etc.). Beneath the comic self-caricature of the lazy, fat philosopher suffering his well-deserved fate, we can also enjoy the truth of his comments as to the necessity of activity for the preservation of good health. He also incidentally reveals much concerning his pleasant life about suburban Passy while he was being lionized by France as he recruited her aid for the American Revolution.

"The Ephemera," an ingenious fable of the short-lived flies, is a poignant, artful look by an old man at the brevity and questionable usefulness of life.

"The Elysian Fields: [a letter from] M. Franklin to Madame Helvetius"—based on its wholeness, richness and brevity—is the best of the lot. It is a masterly, swift, romantic fantasy with real emotion and appeal clothed in the late medieval ideal of courtly love, and the neoclassical device of a dialog in heaven between philosophers. Yet all this is given an American short-story compression in an imaginative entity of two pages, complete with a hard-hitting surprise ending. The reader will notice how quickly Franklin sets up the situation at the beginning:

> Vexed by your barbarous resolution, announced so positively last evening, to remain single all your life in respect to your dear [late] husband, I went home, fell on my bed, and, believing myself dead, found myself in the Elysian Fields.[30]

After the skillful little plot unfolds, the reader will likewise note how quickly, yet powerfully, Franklin ends it, revealing beneath the banter the reality of his love for the widow Helvetius: "Here I am! [Back from heaven, where I found out about the loyalty of our former spouses.] Let us revenge ourselves."

To fill out his little packet of bagatelles, Franklin included with them two essays of a different sort, each worthy of publication in itself, yet directed to other purposes. "Information to Those Who Would Remove to America" is a skillful pamphlet for European prospective emigrants to America, helpful in puncturing false myths of immediate wealth, especially for genteel types, available there; and simultaneously effective in recruiting skilled artisans who were quite in demand and who could expect to make a good living (but no unearned fortunes) in the growing economies of the new states. The other essay, "Remarks Concerning the Savages of North America," is also an indirect recruiting leaflet, to alleviate emigrants' fears as to the brutality of the Indians. Yet it is also a moving essay recognizing the differences between the Indian and white cultures—and the basic civility and dignity of that of the so-called savages.

Our laborious manner of life compared with theirs, they esteem slavish and base; and the learning on which we value ourselves they regard as frivolous and useless. An instance of this occurred at the Treaty of Lancaster in Pennsylvania, Anno 1744, between the Government of Virginia and the Six Nations. [Franklin describes an offer of the whites to educate six Indian youths at William and Mary College.] .'. their speaker began by expressing their deep sense of the kindness of the Virginia government, in making them that offer; for we know, says he, that you highly esteem the kind of learning taught in those colleges, and that the maintenance of our young men while with you, would be very expensive to you. . . . But . . . we have had some experience of it: Several of our young people were formerly brought up at the colleges of the northern provinces; they were instructed in all your sciences; but when they came back to us, they were bad runners, ignorant of every means of living in the woods, unable to bear either cold or hunger, knew neither how to build a cabin, take a deer, or kill an enemy, spoke our language imperfectly; were therefore neither fit for hunters, warriors, or counsellors; they were totally good for

29

nothing. . . . however . . . if the gentlemen of Virginia will send us a dozen of their sons, we will take care of their education, instruct them in all we know, and make *men* of them.[31].

A little examination of this passage will reveal not only Franklin the social commentator and humanitarian-philosopher, but Franklin the writer, putting eloquent English phraseology in the mouth of his semifictional Indian chief.

Clearly, in the "Remarks" essay, the Indian culture is described as more sensible and respectable than the white. The civility, courtesy, kindness and hospitality of all "barbarous" peoples, especially the Indians, are celebrated with resounding examples. Here we see the philosopher Franklin (another one of his masks) at his most benign, anticipating the science of anthropology in recognizing each culture in its own terms. Yet perhaps too, in the land where the "noble savage" was first enunciated by men who had never seen one, Franklin was writing something that he knew would sell.

Other significant writings: Among his other writing of historical, political, economic or scientific interest are many short works, proposals, essays and personal as well as scientific letters. The following are of the most significant political proposals.

1. "Plan for a Union of the English Colonies in America" (1754), also called "The Albany Plan of Union." Under pressure of renewed war with France and her Indian allies, the colonies sent representatives to Albany, New York, to attempt to unite and coordinate their defense efforts. Of the several plans for consolidation proposed, Franklin's was the best, proposing, essentially, dominion status and self-determination for the American colonies, under the British crown. It was passed by the Albany congress but turned down by both the individual colonies (as being too centralized) and by London (for granting too much power to the colonies). Nevertheless, it was a simple-appearing yet sophisticated plan fusing the next

steps needed in both the American colonies and the British empire at large (i.e., unification, and the invention of the commonwealth, respectively).

2. "The Interests of Great Britain Considered" (1760). This direct appeal to the homeland authorities argued for Britain to take Canada, rather than the slave and sugar islands of Guadeloupe, from the French, in the ensuing expected victory, in order to insure much more productive growth for both America and Britain. Franklin, in these and other works, clearly emerges as a prime British-American empire builder and advocate of practical geopolitics for free British institutions.

In addition to his population essay and other economic writings, a wide range of scientific and technological writing shows Franklin's interested and creative mind thinking constructively in dozens of areas. "Experiments and Observations on Electricity" and other papers coin such electrical terms as *positive* and *negative, battery, armature* and *condenser* and outline his famous kite-and-key experiment, identifying lightning as electricity. These papers not only contribute substantial discoveries to the knowledge of man but they reflect anew Franklin's twin abilities (1) to use simple, everyday things from his environment to pursue knowledge and thus make improvements and (2) to write in a few words and with homely examples the material he had on his mind.

Other works chart and study the Gulf Stream (to save English ships two weeks time in their crossing!), advocate crop insurance, analyze how to cure smoky chimneys, suggest daylight saving time as an economy measure (the son of the candlemaker computed the cost of unnecessary candles to the city of Paris), and recommend gypsum as fertilizer in America. He introduced several agricultural improvements, including Newtown Pippin apples in England, and rhubarb, kale and Swiss barley in America. He observed that darker colored clothes absorbed more heat than lighter ones and proved it scientifically by laying out varicolored clothpatches on the snow and seeing the sun melt the snow in varying depths. (In the same letter he proposed six applications of this new knowledge.)[32] He analyzed cyclones and waterspouts; cooling by evaporation (even to the point of refrigeration); comparative conductivity of heat in metals and other substances; sound in air, water, wood and a vacuum; rivers' losses by evaporation; the interaction of fresh water and salt water in estuaries and tidal basins; mammoth tusks and teeth from the Ohio; exploding meteors as sources of sound; and so on. He speculated on hypnotism, the causes of the northern lights, the formation of the earth, the theory of the conservation of energy, and whether the earth carries with it a sphere of hotter air or heat-energy as it journeys around the sun. He witnessed man's first hot-air balloon flights near Paris and prophesied aerial navigation and its use in war. (Ironically, he believed it would reduce war because he thought no monarch could keep enemy troops—two per balloon—from invading his country en masse.)[33] In a letter to Priestley, in 1780, Franklin foresaw, through the discoveries and application of science, the conquest of all diseases, and the possibility that, "We may perhaps learn to deprive large masses of their gravity, and give them absolute levity, for the sake of easy transport." Jules Verne and H. G. Wells would have been highly compatible writers to Franklin. His inventions of course include the lightning rod, bifocals, the better stove, a better-ventilated street lamp and a musical instrument of glass bell-jars which he called the armonica.[34]

Organizational ideas (not limited to governmental ones) were constantly springing up from his fertile mind to solve particular problems. Examples include paving districts (subscribed to by the benefactors thereof), fire departments, police departments, circulating libraries, the first city hospital in America, matching funds from colony and city, local organization to found an academy, cultural clubs for discussions of great books or issues, scientific societies, abolitionist societies, and bequests for civic improvements. An example of the latter—and of Franklin's excited, optimistic view of the future—is the fact that he left a thousand pounds sterling ($5,000) each to the cities of Boston and Philadelphia to be put in credit unions to aid young married artificers set up their own businesses at five percent interest. Further, these funds— to be managed by the town selectmen "united with the ministers of the oldest Episcopalian, Congregational and Presbyterian churches in that town"[35]—were to build up over the years so that $500,000 would be available and put to worthwhile civic use after one hundred years, the remainder to build up again and a larger amount be put to such uses in *two* hundred years! Few men have that great a civic regard, that great an interest, that great a faith in the exhilarating reality of the future.

Franklin, then, as he was a doer in many fields, was also a significant writer in several genres. A great borrower of ideas (an originator of some), but above all a user of ideas, a salesman of brainstorms through skillful design of his work and simplicity and clarity of phrase, a catalyst of himself and other men to action through the written word, he was, in short, a writer who moved his world and who still moves ours. He can be enjoyed for his *Autobiography*, his Poor Richard maxims, his satires and hoaxes, his interesting ideas, his bold and farsighted (even world-shaking) propaganda and persuasion, his advocacy of freedom and justice, his humor and kindness, and his wise and tolerant heart. Though his several other spectacular careers—as statesman, diplomat, revolutionist, economist, scientist, inventor—have masked his literary talents from us, Benjamin Franklin was essentially what David Hume assessed him to be in 1762: America's "first philosopher, and indeed the first great man of letters for whom we are beholden to her."[36]

II

John Adams

John Adams
America's Unrecognized Writer

Men of letters must have a great deal of praise, and some
of the necessaries, conveniences, and ornaments of life.
John Adams
Defence of the Constitutions of
the United States of America (1787-88)

John Adams of Massachusetts (1735-1826), second president of the United States, is not only one of America's least
appreciated presidents; he is also one of America's least
appreciated significant writers. Like the other great stars on
the Revolutionary stage (Franklin, Jefferson, Washington,
Hamilton and Madison), John Adams was able to pack an
astounding amount of worthwhile writing in among the events
and vicissitudes of an arduous legal, diplomatic and political
career. Though not a writer of novels, short stories or plays, he
produced no less than ten volumes of diaries, letters, essays

and state papers, many of them outstanding contributions to constitutional theory, satire and social comment. Yet, while being one of America's most productive early writers, he was also achieving the following remarkable life.

As early as 1755 (at age twenty, the same year he graduated from Harvard) John Adams saw the necessity of a union of the colonies and the inevitability of American independence. He became a teacher and lawyer (after rejecting the ministry as a career) in Braintree—now Quincy—Massachusetts. In 1764 he married Abigail Smith and eventually had five children. He became a leader and writer in the resistance to the Stamp Act (No taxation without representation!). He opposed (in Boston) the presence of British troops in that city and the new jurisdiction of admiralty courts over her affairs. (Yet he refused a lucrative British appointment to those same courts.) In spite of his antipathy to British tyranny, he served, in the interests of preserving law, as lawyer for Captain Thomas Preston, the British officer tried for the Boston "massacre"; Adams won acquittal for his client. In spite of this unpopular move, Adams was supported politically by his powerful second cousin, the fiery militant, Samuel Adams. Furthermore, John was an active member of the Sons of Liberty and 'approved highly of the Boston "Tea Party."

In 1774 and 1776 John Adams was appointed delegate to the First and Second Continental Congresses and played a leading role in getting the various colonies to draw up new constitutions independent of the British crown. He was instrumental in getting Washington appointed commander of the Continental Army (over New England's Hancock—to solidify the Virginia-New England alliance). Later Adams was appointed chief justice of Massachusetts and served in this post for a short time. Outside of his later presidency, he is perhaps best known for being appointed to the Declaration of Independence Committee. There he, according to his side of the story, insisted that Jefferson be the principal author—again in an effort to enlist the Virginians' whole hearts in the cause. After war broke out, Adams served as chairman of the "Board of War and Ordnance" of the Continental Congress—the equivalent of a war minister for the American Revolution.

Adams began his long efforts at diplomacy upon being appointed to join Franklin in France in order to secure American interests and French aid during the Revolution. Upon returning home, he was elected delegate to the Massachusetts State Constitutional Convention (1779) and served as chief framer of the 1780 document. He also wrote most of Massachusetts Bill of Rights, which was later copied by many other states. Again Adams was sent back to Europe as a diplomat. There, working independently of Franklin, he gained badly needed treaties and loans from the Dutch in 1780. Later he was commissioned diplomat to Britain, along with Franklin and Jay, for negotiating the peace treaty ending the Revolutionary War. Excellent terms were obtained for the fledgling country by these veteran diplomats. Independence was granted; the trans-Appalachian territory clear to the Mississippi was ceded; fishing rights off the Newfoundland banks were recognized; and provisions were made for the settlement of debts and the resumption of trade. Eight years of tenacious war and tenacious diplomacy had won the colonies this triumph; and Adams stayed on in France as negotiator of trade treaties for two more years.

He next was appointed first United States ambassador to England and served from 1785 to 1788. However, he achieved little during that period other than writing in 1786 and 1787 his *Defence of the Constitutions of the United States of America*, a work which was highly influential among the delegates to the United States Constitutional Convention in the summer of 1787. His basic concept of check-and-balance "mixed" government emerged throughout the resulting constitution, and he thus gave it his hearty support. Adams was elected vice-president under Washington (1789-97) and thus became the first president of the United States Senate. He was the first to recognize from experience the difficult semipowerlessness of the vice-presidential position in the American governmental design.

Adams is best known, of course, for following Washington in the presidency, and preceding Jefferson; and he has inevitably suffered by comparison. During the difficult period of his administration (1797-1801) he maintained his own and Washington's policy of "no entangling alliances" with war-torn Europe. He thus kept the struggling, infant nation out of France and Britain's wars in spite of three hundred U.S. ship seizures by the French (and almost as many by the British) and strong U.S. factions supporting each side (led by Jefferson and Hamilton, respectively). Adams created a Navy Department to meet the crisis but took strong independent action to negotiate a peace settlement (to the secret war) with France in 1800. His last important act as president was the appointment of John Marshall as chief justice of the Supreme Court—Marshall, who did so much to make the Supreme Court what it has become in the great, flexible check-and-balance government of the United States.

Adams lost the incredibly close election battle (1801) with Jefferson and Aaron Burr. But Hamilton's generous break of the Jefferson-Burr electoral tie achieved the first peaceful change of party administration in United States history, established the two-party system in this country, and set a vital precedent for future peaceful succession in the United States. At sixty-five Adams retired to his farm in Quincy. Later, after Jefferson also retired from office in 1809, Adams became reconciled to his younger opponent, and the two ex-presidents carried on for many years a wise and benign correspondence. During the 1811-1826 period, Adams performed well the role of elder statesman. After the War of 1812, he served as delegate to help revise the Massachusetts Constitution which he had helped design forty years before. In 1825, at eighty-nine years of age, he received the news that his son, John Quincy Adams, already our most successful secretary of state, had been elected president of the United States. Then, as if in commemoration of the Declaration of Independence, John Adams died on the same day as did Jefferson—July 4,

1826—fifty years to the day after both had signed that historic document.

There is no doubt that most of the value in John Adams's extensive writings is based on their historical, biographical and constitutional interest. The works of a "founding father" of the United States—and the only president to have a son who also became president—naturally hold an interest which cannot be fully separated from his public service achievements. But it is the belief of this writer that the literary artist among lawyers and politicians often emerges as the more effective mover of other men (the more powerful aristocrat, even in a republic, as John Adams would say), the more successful statesman, due to his ability to write and think with superior art. Indeed, Gilbert Chinard suggests that, had America been an already established nation with a fully developed culture, John Adams would more likely have emerged as an essayist, satirist or novelist than a political leader and builder of constitutions, treaties and nation.

> Had [Adams] been born in Paris, the boy who at twenty could write with such "verve" would have been hailed as a wit of the first class, and would have been encouraged to develop his rare talent; but neither Worcester nor Boston constituted a favorable milieu in which literary geniuses could grow and receive appreciation and applause, and Adams himself employed all possible effort to suppress . . . his too ready disposition to ridicule, to mock and to satirize. Fortunately for us, he was never able entirely to suppress his "righteous indignation," and whenever occasion presented itself gave vent to his feelings, often much to his damage, but most of the time for our great enjoyment.[1]

In spite of Chinard's comment, however, John Adams's writing frequently was not an impediment to his career (except when he was impolitically forthright in the *Discourses on*

Davila, 1791). Usually, especially up through 1787, Adams's writing was one of the basic supports for that career. And his long studies as a scholar, lawyer and diarist helped him to perfect his thinking as well as his writing ability, sharpened his eye for analysis and detail, and made him a student of men as well as of their institutions. "A pen is certainly an excellent instrument to fix a man's attention and to enflame his ambition."[2] This statement from Adams's diary can certainly be read as that of a political propagandist applying his writer's art to his readers. Yet it can also, and probably more accurately, be read as a writer's contemplation of the voluntary pursuit of his art, building his own personal ability to think and express and thus cause himself to become a power, or, more accurately, a determined and effective will.

It must be admitted that John Adams's ten volumes must be culled to one for most modern readers. He was too complete in his legalistic marshalling of examples from classical authorities to be enjoyable *en toto,* even when setting forth important constitutional principles. Skillful selection of Adams's scattered literary nuggets has probably best been done by Adrienne Koch and William Peden in their interesting dual anthology, *The Selected Writings of John and John Quincy Adams* (1946). Consequently, the bulk of the passages referred to in this chapter and in the chapter on John Quincy Adams are from Koch and Peden's selections. The book is an admirable yet sufficient revelation of the minds and literary art of this distinguished father and son. It is prefaced by an outstanding thirty-three-page introduction entitled, "John Yankee and His Son."

That John Adams considered himself to be a man of letters can be attested to by the quotation opening this essay, as well as by the fact that he frequently wrote far more in his thorough lawyer fashion than the occasion required; witness three volumes on the *Defence* when one was all that was needed. That he was a man of letters in actuality can be sensed by the reader in Adams's effortless devotion to the ringing phrase, the sharp image, the incisive metaphor, the acidic or satiric tone.

John Adams's works may be pursued chronologically through his career or separated into types such as are sketched and sampled here: early letters, diaries, main works (other than state papers), and later letters. Even the letters have frequently been published separately (along with the other side of the correspondence) in works such as the *Warren-Adams Letters* (1917-25); *Familiar Letters of John Adams to his Wife Abigail* (1876); the [later] *Correspondence of Adams and Jefferson*, edited by Paul Wilstach (1925); and the complete *Adams-Jefferson Letters*, edited by Lester Cappon (1959).

Let us look at some of his exemplary early letters.

John Adams's letter to Nathan Webb of October 12, 1755, (written while the great war between France and England for North America and the world was going on) is a fine early sample of young Adams's ability to see and to write. This was the year Adams graduated from Harvard, fourteenth in a class of twenty-four. After discussing how continuous change affects the rise and fall of empires, he writes:

Soon after the Reformation, a few people came over into this new world for conscience' sake. Perhaps this apparently trivial incident may transfer the great seat of empire into America. It looks likely to me: for if we can remove the turbulent Gallicks, our people, according to the exactest computations, will in another century become more numerous than England itself. [He probably reflects a reading of Franklin's essay on population here.] Should this be the case, since we have, I may say, all the naval stores of the nation in our hands, it will be easy to obtain the mastery of the seas; and then the united force of all Europe will not be able to subdue us. The only way to keep us from setting up for ourselves is to disunite us. *Divide et impera.* Keep us in distinct colonies, and then,

41

some great men in each colony desiring the monarchy of the whole, they will destroy each other's influence and keep the country *in equilibrio.*[3]

Here we see the political acumen, foresight and independent mind of the young individual. He is predicting the likely emergence of the United States as *the* world power. Yet he is also implying the colonies' need meantime to unite into one nation and gain independence from Britain in order to meet this bright destiny.

In his letter to Mercy Warren, January 8, 1776, he says, "Politics . . . is the science of human happiness," an aphorism which explains much about his lifelong devotion to the public business and effective representative government despite his misgivings about man's virtue and dependability. In this letter he goes on to show how a republic is much to be preferred over a monarchy. Yet he doubts whether men anywhere, even in America, are virtuous enough to make a republic work.

> Virtue and simplicity of manners are indispensably necessary in a republic among all orders and degrees of men. But there is so much rascality, so much venality and corruption, so much avarice and ambition, such a rage for profit and commerce among all ranks and degrees of men even in America, that I sometimes doubt whether there is public virtue enough to support a republic. There are two vices most detestably predominant in every part of America that I have yet seen which are as incompatible with the spirit of a commonwealth as light is with darkness: I mean servility and flattery. A genuine republican can no more fawn and cringe than he can domineer. Show me the American who cannot do all. I know two or three, I think, and very few more. However, it is the part of a great politician to make the character of his people, to extinguish among them the follies and vices that he

sees, and to create in them the virtues and abilities which he sees wanting. I wish I was sure that America has one such politician but I fear she has not....[4]

On July 3, 1776, John wrote to Abigail telling her that the essential resolution approving the Declaration of Independence was passed the day before. He sings praises for the great brave idea—though not without seeing the dangers and slowness thereof. We lost Canada for not doing it wholeheartedly seven months ago, he says. Yet "a greater [question]... never was nor will be decided among men."

> The second day of July, 1776 will be the most memorable epocha in the history of America ... [;] it will be celebrated by succeeding generations as a great anniversary festival....
> You will think me transported with enthusiasm, but I am not. I am well aware of the toil, and blood, and treasure that it will cost us to maintain this Declaration, and support and defend these States. Yet, through all the gloom, I can see the rays of ravishing light and glory. I can see that the end is more than worth all the means, and that posterity will triumph in that day's transaction, even although we should rue it, which I trust in God we shall not.[5]

On May 3, 1777, in writing to his friend James Warren, Adams showed his inspiring zest that America win her own liberty, not whiningly wait for France to fight England and win America's independence for her. He considered the latter course not only unmanly and weak-willed but compromising our independence with obligations to Europe and endangering America the more by wider involvement in Europe's wars. "The surest and only way to secure her [France's] arms in this cause is for us to exert our own."

I am more concerned about our revenue than the aid of France. Pray let the loan offices do their part, that we may not be compelled to make paper money as plenty and of course as cheap as oak leaves. There is so much injustice in carrying on a war with a depreciating currency that we can hardly pray with confidence for success.[6]

Adams was here rightly pointing out a danger that did indeed almost kill the infant in its crib, one which was not overcome until about 1820, undercapitalization of the whole national enterprise by its people.

From Europe he wrote across the sea to Abigail in 1780 (no date given) a rich comment on the relationship of political and military development to the progress of culture and education. He sketched briefly the rich culture of France, which he did not have time to study or describe (as he would have done twenty-five years before) because his mind was too full of anxiety and the problems of doing his diplomatic job.

The science of government is my duty to study...I must study politics and war, that my sons may have liberty to study mathematics and philosophy. My sons ought to study mathematics and philosophy, geography, natural history, and naval architecture, navigation, commerce, and agriculture, in order to give their children a right to study painting, poetry, music, architecture, statuary, tapestry and porcelain. Adieu.[7]

Two of John Adams's most radical, optimistic and forward-looking quotations occur in letters he wrote in 1785 and 1786 to Count Sarsfield, a genial nobleman who had instructed Adams in court etiquette during his stay in Holland. Judging from the tone and subject matter of the letters, Sarsfield must have been as liberal an aristocrat as Lafayette or Tocqueville.

It has ever been my hobby-horse to see rising in America an empire of liberty, and a prospect of two or three hundred millions of freemen, without one noble or one king among them. You say it is impossible. If I should agree with you in this, I would still say, let us try the experiment, and preserve our equality as long as we can. A better system of education for the common people might preserve them long. . . .[8]

In an earlier letter to Sarsfield, discussing nobility and privileges, Adams closes with this colorful revolutionary blast:

I believe this many-headed beast, the people, will, some time or other, have wit enough to throw their riders; and if they should, they will put an end to an abundance of tricks with which they are now curbed and bitted, whipped and spurred.[9]

What a clear forecast of the French and other revolutions. Yet as we look at it from here, this thought seems far more hopeful than Adams usually was concerning the people.[10] Adams, in his later years seeing the destruction of the French Revolution and the Napoleonic Wars (and their monarchical reaction), felt far less sanguine about the automatic good of revolutions.

Later the same year (1785) he showed his basic Federalism in a letter to John Jay, then Secretary of Foreign Affairs, favoring a stronger unification of the States and more aggressive protectionist trade policies, to enable the United States to survive.

These means can never be secured entirely, until Congress shall be made supreme in foreign commerce, and shall have digested a plan for all the States. . . . It would be infinitely better to have all American ships and seamen entitled to equal privileges in all the thirteen States; but their privileges should be made much greater than those of foreign ships and seamen.[11]

Thus did Adams push, from his post in London, for repair of the basic flaws in the Articles of Confederation.

Let us turn now from samples of his letters to passages from his diaries and more formal works, before returning to close with samples from his later correspondence.

John Adams's diary, kept sporadically from 1755 to 1796, though fragmentary and unpolished, provides a vast source of glimpses of early American life, many anecdotes, portraits, and much soul-searching by the young man as to what would be his destiny. Also, its later European sections present many of John Adams's often naive impressions of the courts of Europe and her cities (Amsterdam, London, Paris) and his fellow diplomats (Franklin, Jay, and young Jefferson) during those exciting days of his diplomacy. These diaries, completely re-edited and annotated, were published anew in 1961 under the editorship of L. H. Butterfield; and they provide a wealth of information on Adams's role in the birth of a nation.

On March 15, 1756, at twenty-one, he wrote in his diary a fine description of himself as teacher-dictator of his little schoolroom kingdom—and of the joys and power of teaching. The psychoanalyst might find the power-hungry leader here.

I sometimes in my sprightly moments consider myself, in my great chair at school, as some dictator at the head of a commonwealth. In this little state I can discover all the great geniuses, all the surprising actions and revolutions of the great world, in miniature. I have several re-nowned generals but three feet high, and several deep projecting politicians in petticoats. I have others catching and dissecting flies, accumulating remarkable pebbles, cockle shells, &c., with as ardent curiosity as any virtuoso in the Royal Society. Some rattle and thunder out A, B,

C, with as much fire and impetuosity as Alexander fought, and very often sit down and cry as heartily upon being outspelt as Caesar did when at Alexander's sepulchre he recollected that the Macedonian hero had conquered the world before his age. At one table sits Mr. Insipid, foppling and fluttering, spinning his whirligig, or playing with his fingers, as gaily and wittily as any Frenchified coxcomb brandishes his cane or rattles his snuffbox. At another, sits the polemical divine, plodding and wrangling in his mind about "Adam's fall, in which we sinned all," as his Primer has it. In short, my little school, like the great world, is made up of kings, politicians, divines, L.D.'s, fops, buffoons, fiddlers, sycophants, fools, coxcombs, chimney sweepers, and every other character drawn in history, or seen in the world. Is it not, then, the highest pleasure, my friend, to preside in this little world, to bestow the proper applause upon virtuous and generous actions, to blame and punish every vicious and contracted trick, to wear out of the tender mind every thing that is mean and little, and fire the new-born soul with a noble ardor and emulation? The world affords no greater pleasure.[12]

This passage reveals much about the man, as well as the boys—and one of the basic attractions in the teaching profession, if we honestly analyze and reveal our feelings as Adams was doing.

On May 17, 1756, he wrote in his diary a striking paragraph on the power of man's knowledge when applied and organized:

The elephant and the lion, when their strength is directed and applied by man, can exert a prodigious force. But their strength, great and surprising as it is, can produce no great effects when applied by no higher ingenuity than their own. But man, although the powers of his body are but small and contemptible, by the exercise of his reason can invent engines and instruments, to take advantage of the powers in nature, and accomplish the most astonishing designs. He can rear the valley into a lofty mountain, and reduce the mountain to a humble vale. He can rend the rocks and level the proudest trees; at his pleasure the forest is cleared, the palaces rise; when he pleases, the soaring eagle is precipitated to earth, and the light-footed roe is stopped in his career. He can cultivate and assist nature in her own productions, by pruning the trees and manuring the land. He makes the former produce larger and fairer fruit; and the latter to bring forth better and greater plenty of grain. He can form a communication between remotest regions for the benefit of trade and commerce, over the yielding and fluctuating element of water. The telescope has settled the regions of heaven, and the microscope has brought up to view innumerable millions of animals that escape the observation of our naked sight.[13]

Here we have a writer, an artist who uses the rhythms of the King James English to express the wonders of technology, reason and organization in the great future arena, America. Such appreciation of man's potentials has been part of America's dynamism from the start of English settlements to the present; and the man who can make his thoughts sing on paper is a writer.

An entry from his diary on December 18, 1760 reads in part: "Lawyers live upon the sins of the people. . . . In short, vice and folly are so interwoven in all human affairs that they could not, possibly, be wholly separated from them without tearing and rending the whole system of human nature and state; nothing would remain as it is."[14]

Here we have an eloquent contemplation, giving pause to the reader as it did to Adams of the totally world-shattering possibilities of man if somehow all were to become virtuous.

The unlikelihood of complete virtue ever arriving causes the practical Puritan to renew his studies of ways government might hold in check man's ever-renewing greed and aggression.

On January 30, 1768, four years after his marriage, three years after the Stamp Act propelled him into politics, six months after the birth of his first son, John Quincy, John Adams wrote in his diary:

> To what object are my views directed? What is the end and purpose of my studies, journeys, labors of all kinds, of body and mind, of tongue and pen? Am I grasping at money or scheming for power? Am I planning the illustration of my family or the welfare of my country? These are great questions. In truth, I am tossed about so much from post to pillar that I have not leisure and tranquillity enough to consider distinctly my own views, objects, and feelings. I am mostly intent, at present, upon collecting a library; and I find that a great deal of thought and care, as well as money, are necessary to assemble an ample and well-chosen assortment of books. But, when this is done, it is only a means, an instrument. Whenever I shall have completed my library, my end will not be answered. Fame, fortune, power, say some, are the ends intended by a library. The service of God, country, clients, fellow men, say others. Which of these lie nearest my heart? . . .
>
> I am certain, however, that the course I pursue will neither lead me to fame, fortune, power, nor to the service of my friends, clients, or country. . . .[15]

The value of these thoughts are their universal application to men and women. They are basic questions of life which many never ask and to which few find satisfactory answers. Adams here is the conscientious, church-going man asking himself, "Am I working selfishly for power and fame or selflessly for service and productivity to others?" Yet in his usual pessimism he is certain he will achieve neither. Or is he simply being modest for posterity? Notice that he is keeping it in a diary which he will save for the rest of his life. Or perhaps, like a personification of practical Puritanism (a bit like Franklin), he is implying that a fusion of both aims is not only possible, but necessary, in the successful man.

For December 17, 1773, there is a passage eloquently praising the Boston "Tea Party" as so bold, daring, firm, intrepid and inflexible "that I cannot but consider it as an epocha in history. . . . To let it be landed would be giving up the principle of taxation by parliamentary authority, against which the continent has struggled for ten years."[16]

Six months later, on June 25, 1774, he was not so euphoric as he recorded the fears and resolves of a thoughtful man pondering war.

> Since the Court adjourned without day this afternoon, I have taken a long walk through the Neck, as they call it, a fine tract of land in a general field. Corn, rye, grass, interspersed in great perfection this fine season. I wander alone and ponder. I muse, I mope, I ruminate. I am often in reveries and brown studies. The objects before me are too grand and multifarious for my comprehension. We have not men fit for the times. We are deficient in genius, in education, in travel, in fortune, in everything. I feel unutterable anxiety. God grant us wisdom and fortitude! Should the opposition be suppressed, should this country submit, what infamy and ruin! God forbid. Death in any form is less terrible![17]

Here is the thirty-nine-year-old New England lawyer, not sorry for the rumbling surge toward independence, but clearly facing the possibility of disaster for the colonial militants.

Adams's chief works beyond the diaries include the "Dissertation on the Canon and Feudal Law," a militant editorial championing America as a land breaking free from old world tyrannies of religious and aristocratic privilege. Originally written in February, 1765, as an essay on church and state tyranny for his Boston lawyers' club, it was published in August in the Boston *Gazette* and reprinted in England under the title given above. This document of a dozen pages deserves to be read in its entirety. It is a great, little-known battle cry for freedom—an assertion that such freedom is a natural right. It is an announcement to Europe that America, through her birth, settlement and growth, has come to be committed against both canonical and aristocratic tyranny. There are many eloquent lines; and clear principles are declared, among them the right of the people to inquire into the character and conduct of their rulers. It briskly asserts America's devotion to both religious and civil freedom and the necessity of education and initiative to protect both. It advocates taxation in proportion to wealth for the vital public education. Freedom of the press is a fact now in America and is a right which should be protected. The freedom to think, question authority and assert conclusions is vital to the rights of man. "Let us dare to read, think, speak and write."[18] This fiery pamphlet will surprise readers who think of John Adams as a conservative.

Another vigorous work from 1765 is Adams's "Instructions of the Town of Braintree to Their Representative." This was a strong resolution in response to the Stamp Act, adopted by the selectmen of his town and forty other towns in Massachusetts to legally resist that "unconstitutional tax." Here we see Adams's sophisticated understanding of constitutional principles emerging among those upstart colonists from the backwoods of America. The enlargement of this sense of constitutionality was perhaps, next to separation of church and state, America's greatest contribution to good government. "We have always understood it to be a grand and fundamental principle *of the constitution* [italics added] that no freeman should be subject to any tax to which he has not given his own consent, in person or by proxy."[19] Adams and his friends (Otis, Hancock, Samuel Adams, and later Jefferson and Wythe) were thus requiring Britain to formulate a clearer definition of her own vague constitution through the use of the basic principle of democracy, no taxation without representation. (The principle was of course an advanced English invention.) Adams also eloquently resisted the enforcement of this Stamp Act through juryless admiralty courts whose judges were paid by commissions on guilty-verdict fines. He asserted the classic idea of rights for the colonists equal to those of free Britons at home—the very nub of the American Revolution: representation in Parliament or (preferably) their own representative assemblies' right to approve or veto this tax and all taxes. He instructed the representatives further not to allow any public expenditure (in the colonies) to carry out the enforcement of this unconstitutional law.

In the "Novanglus Papers," published in the Boston *Gazette* from December, 1774, to April, 1775, Adams replied to a series of articles by Judge Daniel Leonard. Leonard, a Tory, had signed himself, "Massachusettensis" in appealing to "the good people of Massachusetts" to be loyal to the king and respect the law.[20] Adams's replies, totalling 166 pages when later published in book form, asserted with passion the rights of Massachusetts people (New England) to govern themselves without interference from crown or Parliament. Chinard says that some of these replies were lost before printing but that we should not mourn as " 'Novanglus' is a heavy, pedantic, ill-composed dissertation ... " written

> to prove that colonization, as such, has no legal status, and that the laws of England cannot extend beyond the sea. ... Unfortunately he was more occupied with the minute refutation of Massachusettensis' arguments than his own thesis.[21]

The "Novanglus Papers," despite Chinard's dim view of them, include some stirring passages:

I would ask, by what law the Parliament has authority over America? By the law of God, in the Old and New Testament, it has none; by the law of nature and nations, it has none; by the common law of England, it has none, for the common law, and the authority of Parliament founded on it, never extended beyond the four seas; by statute law it has none, for no statute was made before the settlement of the colonies for this purpose; and the declaratory act, made in 1766, was made without our consent. . . . And how shall this defect be supplied? It cannot be supplied consistently with reason, justice, policy, morality, or humanity without the consent of the colonies and *some new plan of connection* [italics added].[22]

Here in 1774-75 was another clear voice from the colonies, warlike, yet firm, with the kind of constitutional analysis that was forcing Britain to improve and articulate more clearly her own constitution, or lose the colonies forever.

A more influential paper was the brief "Thoughts on Government" of January, 1776. It was a plan of republican government written at the request of Virginia's George Wythe, to help him and all the colonies troubled by the problems of constructing new state governments to replace the colonial ones. It was strong in advocating his principle of mixed or balanced-power-group government, which has certainly come to be the central principle in the 200-year viability of the United States of America. Adams said he wrote "Thoughts on Government" to counteract the unicameral system being advocated by Thomas Paine.[23] Richard Henry Lee had Adams's tract printed in pamphlet form, and it was highly influential with Congress and convention delegates during this formative period.

John Adams's role in *not* writing the first draft of the Declaration of Independence (in deference to Jefferson and the Virginians) but in reviewing the draft prior to the rest of the committee and Congress, is well clarified in Adams's letter to Timothy Pickering, August 6, 1822.[24] (See the opening of the chapter on Jefferson for part of this letter.)

John Adams's greatest work, both in size and in influence, was *A Defence of the Constitutions of Government of the United States of America* (1787-88), in three volumes. He started writing this work in England in the fall of 1786, to refute European critics of the American state constitutions and the Articles of Confederation; but in so doing he set forth at length in Volume I his theory of check-and-balance government so well that he had a major influence on the Constitutional Convention, meeting and doing its great work in the summer of 1787.

Two passages will suffice to represent the *Defence of the Constitutions* as to both John Adams's classic views of man and government, and his literary style and pungency. In the preface to Volume I, he writes:

It is become a kind of fashion among writers to admit, as a maxim, that if you could be always sure of a wise, active, and virtuous prince, monarchy would be the best of governments. But this is so far from being admissible that it will forever remain true that a free government has a great advantage over a simple monarchy. The best and wisest prince, by means of a freer communication with his people, and the greater opportunities to collect the best advice from the best of his subjects, would have an immense advantage in a free state over a monarchy. A senate consisting of all that is most noble, wealthy, and able in the nation, with a right to counsel the crown at all times, is a check to ministers, and a security against abuses, such as a body of nobles who never meet, and have no such right, can never supply. Another assembly, composed of representatives chosen by the people in all parts, gives free access to the whole nation, to the government; it excites emulation among all classes, removes complaints, redresses grievances, affords opportunities of all the faculties of man; it opens a passage for every speculation to the legislature, to administration, and to the public; it gives a universal energy to the human character, in every part of the state, such as never can be obtained in a monarchy.[25]

Adams's later critics who accused him of monarchical tendencies based on *Discourses on Davila* should also have recalled this paean for elected, mixed, republican representative government.

After showing that in every society certain aristocratic families emerge to have larger-than-average influence, Adams then ponders how these powerful families and individuals can be kept from dominating all government for their own privilege.

The only remedy is to throw the rich and the proud into one group, in a separate assembly, and there tie their hands; if you give them scope with the people at large or their representatives, they will destroy *all equality and liberty, with the consent and acclamations* of the people themselves. They will have much more power mixed with the representatives than separated from them. In the first case, if they unite, they will give the law and govern all; if they differ, they will divide the state, and go to a decision by force. But placing them alone by themselves, the society avails itself of all their abilities and virtues; they become a solid check to the representatives themselves, as well as to the executive power, and you disarm them entirely of the power to do mischief.[26]

Here is a writer who can make the dry principles of government clear through his art.

A sequel to the *Defence* was *Discourses of Davila* (1791), a volume of political papers written during his first year as vice-president. These essays set forth his essentially conservative political views—now that independence was won. He later

55

wondered at his own temerity in stating his realism and pessimism about man and government so forthrightly. In his own words, "The work . . . powerfully operated to destroy his popularity. It was urged as full proof, that he was an advocate of monarchy, and laboring to introduce a hereditary president in America."[27]

As a sole literary sample of many one might choose from *Discourses on Davila*, an extract from Part III is presented. This is a searing, exquisite analysis of the role of the love of praise in the affairs of men:

> The desire of the esteem of others is as real a want of nature as hunger; and the neglect and contempt of the world as severe a pain as the gout or stone. It sooner and oftener produces despair, and a detestation of existence; of equal importance to individuals, to families, and to nations. It is a principal end of government to regulate this passion. It is the only adequate instrument of order and subordination in society, and alone commands effectual obedience to laws, since without it neither human reason nor standing armies would ever produce that great effect. Every personal quality, and every blessing of fortune, is cherished in proportion to its capacity of gratifying this universal affection for the esteem, the sympathy, admiration, and congratulations of the public. Beauty in the face, elegance of figure, grace of attitude and motion, riches, honors, everything is weighed in the scale, and desired, not so much for the pleasure they afford, as the attention they command.[28]

Thus did John Adams, American thinker and writer, analyze man, seeing clearly how the pursuit of praise, i.e., the pursuit of love, motivates all human beings.

Adams also wrote, between 1802 and 1807, a partial *Autobiography* of some 450 pages (Butterfield edition), covering three phases of his life: (1) Boyhood through 1776; (2) Travels and Negotiations, 1777-1778; and (3) Peace: 1779-

1780. Writing in 1807, he broke off in midsentence in the midst of a 1780 letter from Vergennes and never completed the manuscript. Thus, like Franklin, Adams did not cover in his autobiography all of the most significant times of his life—though plentiful diary entries fill up many of the gaps thus created. The *Autobiography*, although not finished, does present Adams's more reflective views of many significant events, including his trip across poverty-stricken, medieval Spain of 1780.

In returning now to Adams's later correspondence, one might present a large array of interesting examples—from warm letters to Abigail, friendly ones to Benjamin Rush or Benjamin Waterhouse, gentle ones to his critic, Jefferson's economist, John Taylor—many of which add to his lustre as a literary man. But by far the most significant and literary collection of Adams's letters are those he wrote to Thomas Jefferson (in exchange for equally excellent responses from that letter writer extraordinary) as both ex-presidents reconciled their political feuds and re-established the camaraderie of their youthful revolutionary days. Edwin H. Cady has written of this exchange:

> This sunset correspondence is a great one for a number of reasons. Both men were accomplished letter writers, and it seems clear that they put themselves out to impress each other. They had minds richly stocked both with scholarship and significant experience. Since each had contributed importantly to the design of the foundations of the Republic, their reminiscences and interpretations cast authoritative light on our national origins. Finally, they were heroic men—as Jefferson himself put it, Argonauts. That they should deliberately have set out to record their self-explanations so cordially is an event almost without parallel.[29]

One of the best of Adams's contributions to this excellent American book is his letter on religion, in the words of Koch and Peden, "a subject on which they reached substantial agreement. Both are closer to Unitarianism in their thinking than to any other organized religion."[30] Adams wrote:

God has infinite wisdom, goodness, and power; he created the universe; his duration is eternal, *a parte ante* and *a parte post*. His presence is as extensive as space. What is space? An infinite spherical vacuum. He created this speck of dirt and the human species for his glory; and with the deliberate design of making nine tenths of our species miserable for ever for his glory. This is the doctrine of Christian theologians, in general, ten to one. Now, my friend, can prophecies or miracles convince you or me that infinite benevolence, wisdom, and power, created and preserves for a time, innumerable millions, to make them miserable for ever, for his own glory? Wretch! What is his glory? Is he ambitious? Does he want promotion? Is he vain, tickled with adulation, exulting and triumphing in his power and the sweetness of his vengeance? Pardon me, my Maker, for these awful questions. My answer to them is always ready. I believe no such things. My adoration of the author of the universe is too profound and too sincere. The love of God and his creation—delight, joy, triumph, exultation in my own existence—though but an atom, a *molecule organique* in the universe—are my religion.

Howl, snarl, bite, ye Calvinistic, ye Anthanasian divines, if you will; ye will say I am no Christian; I say ye are no Christians, and there the account is balanced. Yet I believe all the honest men among you are Christians, in my sense of the word. . . . [31]

Here, writing in 1813, was a worthy intellectual godfather to Emerson and Mark Twain.

To Hezekiah Niles, publisher of the *Niles Weekly Register* (Baltimore), an important newspaper, John Adams wrote on February 13, 1818, apparently replying to the question, "What was the real American Revolution?" His answer: "This radical change in the principles, opinions, sentiments, and affections of the people was the real American Revolution." He urged that the process be studied by young men of letters (and all records collected and sought out—even down to handbills) to recover as much of the history of this great world-shaking event as was recoverable. This research would be of great importance "to posterity, not only in this nation but in South America and all other countries."

> The complete accomplishment of it [the independence and unification into one new nation] in so short a time and by such simple means, was perhaps a singular example in the history of mankind. Thirteen clocks were made to strike together—a perfection of mechanism which no artist had ever before affected.[32]

Thus we see again that the potential literary artists had become political and diplomatic artists as the occasion required.

John Adams continued then to be literally and figuratively a man of letters on into his seventies and eighties, coining phrases and exploding epithets that still ring in our ears. His life and letters approach their close with his letter to Thomas Jefferson of January 23, 1825. Here in his ninetieth year he gives a great restatement of his belief in freedom of thought and his unalterable opposition to censorship of ideas in the name of the Christian church.[33]

His literary life may be fittingly closed with this brief, passionate paragraph of love, written to his son John Quincy on hearing that the latter had been elected president of the United States.

My dear son, I have received your letter of the 9th. Never did I feel so much solemnity as upon this occasion. The multitude of my thoughts, and the intensity of my feelings are too much for a mind like mine, in its ninetieth year. May the blessing of God Almighty continue to protect you to the end of your life, as it has heretofore protected you in so remarkable a manner from your cradle! I offer the same prayer for your lady and your family, and am your affectionate father.[34]

Note John Adams's final wisdom: he gives no advice.

III

The Quotable Mr. Jefferson

Mr. Jefferson came into Congress, in June, 1775, and brought with him a reputation for literature, science, and a happy talent of composition. Writings of his were handed about, remarkable for the peculiar felicity of expression. . . .

The sub-committee met. Jefferson proposed to me to make the draft. I said, "I will not." "You should do it." "Oh! no." "Why will you not? You ought to do it." "I will not." "Why?" "Reasons enough." "What can be your reasons?" "Reason first—You are a Virginian, and a Virginian ought to appear at the head of this business. Reason second—I am obnoxious, suspected, and unpopular. You are very much otherwise. Reason third—You can write ten times better than I can." "Well," said Jefferson, "if you are decided, I will do as well as I can."

"Very well. When you have drawn it up, we will have a meeting."[1]

John Adams
Letter to Timothy Pickering
August 6, 1822, on the
authorship of the Decla-
ration of Independence.

Thomas Jefferson as republican, democrat, decentralist and champion of freedom is so well known as to need no introduction. Jefferson as Virginia aristocrat, third president, buyer of the Louisiana Territory (800,000 square miles at three cents an acre), patron of Lewis and Clark, as architect, inventor, scientific farmer, educator, slavery-hating slaveholder and American renaissance man is also well known. But Thomas Jefferson as one of the major writers of America (total works—more than fifty volumes) may be somewhat of a surprise to the reader—especially since other than his brief *Notes on Virginia* and his partial *Autobiography* (together little over two hundred pages) he wrote no books. The reason Jefferson is not known as a writer (except as the writer of the Declaration of Independence) is that he was not a producer of books, plays or poems, but was an occasional writer, producing a steady stream of letters, declarations, public statements, laws, speeches, essays and more letters to meet the needs of the hour in his colony, state, diplomatic post or nation. And he had a host of other cultural interests—music, education, languages, architecture, science, farming—which called forth letters of all sorts to all kind of people, strangers as well as friends. His services as statesman and his ideas as a philosopher rightly eclipsed the literary production of the writer, as they were in fact his more important contributions. Yet as a constant doer and a busy occasional writer—as congressman, diplomat, secretary of state, vice-president, president and elder statesman—Jefferson produced thousands of pages (an estimated 50,000 letters for example)[2] reflecting every conceivable subject among his diverse interests: the nature and rights of man; the principles of government; the benefits of science and education; the events of the French Revolution (part of which he witnessed); the design of buildings; what kind of animals mammoths might be—based on the numerous discoveries of their bones; the Anglo-Saxon language as a source for a better understanding of English and English-speaking peoples; Indians—their cultures, traits, languages, migrations, burial customs, and integration into the white society; Negroes—their abilities, grievances, emancipation from slavery, need for education and training and resettlement (since he did not believe integration of the blacks into the white society would work). And his very scattering of his words and ideas in many small units, rather than concentrating them into systematic and fully developed works, requires the reader to hunt out for himself Jefferson's whole expression in any one area. Indeed, many skilled scholars and editors have helped the reader find Thomas Jefferson the writer (Adrienne Koch and William Peden, *Life and Selected Writings of Thomas Jefferson;* Gordon Lee, *Crusade Against Ignorance: Thomas Jefferson on Education;* Saul Padover, *Thomas Jefferson on Democracy;* Paul Wilstach, *Correspondence of Adams and Jefferson*). Yet usually his writing is so inextricably bound up with his heroic and philosophic role in the creation and rescue of the United States (and overshadowed by interest in his ideas for their own sake) that we fail to notice the literary artist at work. Yet that artist is always there, articulating the ideas, and supporting, sustaining, inspiring, indeed making possible the statesman himself.

According to Koch and Peden, when the Second Continental Congress met in 1775:

> Jefferson's happy talent of composition [alluding to Adams's phrase quoted above] seems to have won him the role of writing more bills, reports and official documents than any of his contemporaries. It is generally conceded

that his talent as an organizer and writer of public papers was one of the solid pillars of his statesmanship.[3]

Winning such respect at thirty-two was mainly the result of the reputation he had made a year earlier with his eloquent Thomas Paine-like resolution intended for the First Continental Congress, "A Summary View of the Rights of British America" (1774). Thus we see that as Franklin had done with his 1728 pamphlet on the advantages of paper money for Pennsylvania, as John Adams had done with his youthful "Dissertation on the Canon and Feudal Law," and as John Quincy Adams did later with his Publicola papers, so young Thomas Jefferson gained the attention and respect of his area's leaders with his ability to write a stirring and convincing pamphlet. It is the thesis of this writer that such writing ability, if not mandatory in the executive himself, is required in his administration—and frequently becomes the route by which an unknown man of talent distinguishes himself and becomes an effective leader himself.

Of course, developing during the American Revolutionary age, Jefferson's writing talents, like those of his contemporaries, were spent largely in the great political and theoretical efforts at the separation and establishment of the new republican complex-federal nation. Thus, his writing, beyond a few ringing passages, does not appeal to everyone. But Thomas Jefferson holds electric interest for anyone not repelled by essay and abstract discussion who is also concerned with any of the following:

1. Whether or not man is inherently good, able, just, and competent enough to seek his own and society's best interests. (Jefferson's affirmative answers here lead him to the following concepts.)

2. The inherent (or natural) right of man to self-government.

3. The inherent right of man to protection against aggression by his own institutions: government, church, the military,

excessive debts, even archaic constitutions, republican legislatures, and especially the judiciary.

4. The freedom of the press and the freedom of inquiry.

5. The necessity of protecting dissent and diversity.

6. Decentralization rather than centralization as a basic principle of both government and civilization. (Decentralization was to be sought in the interests of individual freedom, virtue and simplicity—agrarian America being the best America.)

7. Solving slavery—by ending the slave trade, then by emancipation, training and resettlement of blacks.

8. The advancement of science, to discover truths from a study of nature and society. (Jefferson included the social sciences and scholarship in his concept of science.)

9. The necessity of the broadest possible education for the happiness, self-development and freedom of man, as well as for the highest good of society.

10. Americans as a chosen people, the new Israel, given this great opportunity for self-government by a benevolent Creator, that they might lead all men to freedom. This was to be accomplished by the United States proving that freedom is more effective, responsible, economic and powerful than tyranny. (As Chinard points out, it is ironic that Jefferson, the cosmopolitan epicurean aristocrat, would adopt this Puritan idea while John Adams, the Puritan farmer's son, adopted a more European skepticism about the likelihood of democracy's success.)[4] This new Israel idea was, however, the root of the later, more aggressive, American concept of manifest destiny.

Lincoln, who steeped himself in Jefferson, put it simply: "The principles of Jefferson are the definitions and axioms of free society."[5]

It should not be assumed that Jefferson was the great originator of these ideas. English reformers as far back as Wycliffe had indirectly asserted the right of the people to depose a king who was not virtuously serving the good of his people. The whole history of the English nation had put into practice this idea in gradually limiting the powers of the monarchy and asserting first the nobles' and then the people's representative power. Roger Williams had championed in 1644 both the concepts of separation of church and state and the right of the individual to freedom of conscience. John Locke in his *Second Treatise on Government* in 1685 had asserted that, "The end of government is the good of mankind . . . " and the power to legislate reverts to the people "when, by the miscarriages of those in authority it is forfeited."[6] And the concepts of constitutionalism, limitation and separation of government powers, representative democracy and the social compact were well known in English and American law and French governmental theory. The land which had produced the Mayflower Compact, Anne Hutchinson, the Zenger case, Benjamin Franklin and the Albany Plan of Union, James Otis's speech against general search warrants, and George Mason's "Virginia Declaration of Rights" was riddled with men and women opposing the medieval tyrannies of the past. Yet the very fact that even a casual student of intellectual history sees that Jefferson was not a great originator argues that his ability must lie in two related areas: (1) his fresh, brief, inspiring *articulation* of these ever-new ideas (that is, his ability to write); and (2) his ability to get these ideas accepted and in practical use in his time and place and among succeeding generations (for which, see his successful political career and the subsequent history of U.S. civil rights and state-individual relations). Since the second of these two skills invariably requires (from someone) great effectiveness with the first, and since Thomas Jefferson was his own writer, it is fair to say that Thomas Jefferson's ability to write, his "felicity of expression," in John Adams's phrase, was the key, not only to his political success, but to his appeal to later generations of readers.

The "Summary View of the Rights of British America," the

paper which called forth Thomas Jefferson to fame in 1774, is a young man's stirring blast for American independence. It asserts vigorously the following number of ideas:

1. The colonies are not now and never were under the authority of the Parliament of England. "The true ground on which we declare these acts void, is, that the British Parliament has no right to exercise authority over us."[7] Here he advances the idea put forward a decade earlier by James Otis of Boston in his "Rights of the British Colonies" (1764): that Parliament had no right to tax the colonies. In referring to a parliamentary act suspending the legislature of New York, Jefferson writes: "One free and independent legislature, hereby takes upon itself to suspend the powers of another, free and independent as itself."[8] In short, colonies of free Englishmen settling in heretofore wild lands have never been legally accounted for in the British constitution.

2. Government, existing for the use of the people, is therefore subject to their superintendence and correction. The king himself is not above criticism, superintendence and replacement, if necessary, by the people (John Locke's best ideas and an application of the principle of Britain's own "Glorious Revolution" of 1688).

3. Free men have a right to emigrate to and set up homes in another country (as did the Saxons to establish England) "and of there establishing new societies, under such laws and regulations as, to *them*, shall seem most likely to promote public happiness" (italics added).[9] It was this reason which led Chinard to say of the "Summary View": "In some respects it is a more original and more important document than the Declaration of Independence itself."[10] The originality and social revolution he sees in it are the assertions of man's natural right to emigrate and settle unoccupied lands, this right then leading to that of self-government in the new social unit (including the right to taxation only with representation and majority consent), i.e., basic independence of the colony from the country or social unit left, with an inherent right to

settle unused or little-used land. (Landowners corporate and private the world around, beware.) Thus the Anglo-Saxons in England were independent of the Saxon homeland. Jefferson doubtless drew this idea from Franklin's satire of the previous year, "Edict of the Emperor of Prussia" (1773), lampooning a mock German monarch for just as ridiculous an assertion of power over long-established *de facto* independent states (England) as George III was now pressing against "British America." Disregarding ownership or consent rights of any aborigines in the "new habitations," this pair of rights (emigration and settlement sovereignty), if accepted, destroys *en toto* the legitimacy of colonial empires and mercantilism for the benefit of the mother country. The second even yet rumbles with power against wealthy landowners (including the Communist Party) the world over. This is basically the squatters' sovereignty doctrine which emerges later among the Jacksonians, a concept deeply imbedded in Anglo-American law as reflected in riparian water rights and the phrase, "Possession is nine points of the law." Yet Chinard correctly sees Jefferson's originality in enunciating as natural (i.e., moral) any man's right *to move out* of a difficult or badly run country (city, state) if he thinks he can find better opportunities elsewhere. Few totalitarian states today recognize this as a right of each citizen. Yet surely it should be the first and last right of an individual in relation to his government.

4. English colonists in America, Jefferson goes on to assert, settled themselves at their own private expense with no government funds; hence, they have no obligations of a special subservient nature to the crown. It was the independent choice of the colonists to maintain union with the mother country by adopting her laws and her king as executive (implying no legal right of the mother country to dominate them). Thus Jefferson is still forwarding Franklin's 1754 invention of the commonwealth concept (parallel nation-states under a common king) and emphasizing it with such unsubservient terms "British America" and "American States."

5. To Jefferson, Parliament's control of American colonial trade was the worst usurpation of all, especially after she had made a solemn treaty with Virginia in 1651 guaranteeing free trade to the colonies. "An American subject is forbidden to make a hat for himself, of the fur he has taken, perhaps, on his own soil; an instance of despotism, to which no parallel can be produced in the most arbitrary ages of British History."[11]

Thomas Jefferson, the thirty-one-year-old unknown from Shadwell, then specifically takes the king to task for his failures in the proper exercise of his executive power, "the only mediatory power between the several states of the British empire."[12]

He possesses indeed the executive power of the laws in every State; *but they are the laws of the particular State* [italics mine], which he is to administer within that State, and not those of any one within the limits of another.[13]

Besides the right of the people to choose their own king and monitor his performance (the lesson of 1688), Jefferson suggests a number of checks on the king's and Parliament's power. In his view, neither may legally do any of the following:

(*a*) dissolve legislatures—

From the nature of things, every society must, at all times, possess within itself the sovereign powers of legislation. . . . But when they are dissolved, by the lopping off one or more of their branches, the power reverts to the people, who may use it to unlimited extent, either assembling together in person, sending deputies, or in any other way they may think proper.[14]

(*b*) grant lands—"emigrations, settlement, occupancy give title, not kingly grant,"[15]

(*c*) tax the colonies without their consent,

(*d*) restrict their trade,

(*e*) quarter troops among them—"His Majesty has no right to land a single armed man on our shores,"[16]

(*f*) make the civil power subject to the military instead of vice versa.

In light of all these illegal deeds, already done by Britain to her colonies (foreshadowing the Declaration's list of grievances) Jefferson asks most challenging questions: "But can his Majesty thus put down all law under his feet? Can he erect a power superior to that which erected himself?"[17]

Was there ever a European (or British) petition to a king which dared to point out so bluntly the specific failures of the sovereign's recent executive performance?

These are our grievances, which we have thus laid before his Majesty, with that freedom of language and sentiment which becomes a free people claiming their rights as derived from the laws of nature, and not as the gift of their Chief Magistrate. Let those flatter, who fear: it is not an American art. To give praise where it is not due might be well from the venal, but would ill beseem those who are asserting the rights of human nature. They know, and will, therefore, say, that Kings are the servants, not the proprietors of the people. Open your breast, Sire, to liberal and expanded thought....[18]

Such wasted eloquence on George III!

Undoubtedly the tract as a petition was rightly voted down by the Virginia Assembly as too strong to be effectual; but had the British allowed the Americans to teach them to accept such criticism from within and used such to effect real reforms, would not the British empire have availed itself of the strength of flexibility for reform which has taken America so far? Would she not possibly have built the unbeatable English-speaking empire envisioned by Franklin, moving its capital to America in due time? In 1763 perhaps. But by 1774 it was already too late.

The "Rights of British America" as written, unnecessarily insulting in places, is clearly an ultimatum—"This, Sire, is our last, our determined resolution."[19]—and not a bona fide petition for the relief of grievances. It cannot be doubted that Jefferson knew his blast could never be accepted in Britain, much less be acquiesced to by the king; and thus the "Summary View" emerges not as a legitimate petition but as a propaganda salvo for home consumption, for rallying the colonies to resolution and unity. It was being considered for proposal to the First Continental Congress, called when the colonial leaders could see that unified action against parliamentary oppression was vital to their interests. Only the lack of their ripeness as to complete advocacy of independence and the lack of the document's general acceptance by the two respective assemblies for which it was slated prevented it from being the document of fame.

The Declaration of Independence, Jefferson's better-known attempt to legalize revolution, has been called by Saul Padover, "Jefferson's Prose Poem."[20] Carl Becker is more moderate in his praise:

> The Declaration has not the grand manner—that passion under control which lifts prose to the level of true poetry. Yet it has, what is the next best thing, a quality which saves it from falling to the prosaic. It has elevation . . . a high seriousness, a kind of lofty pathos which at least lift the Declaration to the level of a great occasion. These qualities . . . illustrate, in its subtler forms what John Adams called [Jefferson's] "peculiar felicity of expression."[21]

Surely exclusive of its list of grievances, the Declaration is a work of literary art. It includes in its moderate beginning a ringing statement of the ideals of democratic government and the basic goal of successful human relations. It was written almost entirely by Jefferson with a few small improvements and changes by the rest of the committee (Adams, Franklin,

Robert Livingston and Roger Sherman) and Congress itself in debate. These changes are shown in the before-and-after version included in Jefferson's 1821 *Autobiography*.[22] They generally improved it, cutting it a bit in length and height of rhetoric, Adams doubtless inserting the two appeals to "the supreme judge of the world" and "divine providence" which place it more in a religious framework than Jefferson would have done. The latter change made it more in keeping with the views of the majority of that Congress and of the majority of Americans to this day than with the largely secular-legal view Jefferson had maintained in it.

The most significant deletion was that of Jefferson's attack on the king first for permitting the "piratical warfare" and "cruel war against human nature itself," the slave trade (and presumably slavery itself), and second, since slaves had been made legal property in the colonies, for inciting "those very people to rise in arms among us, and to purchase that liberty of which he has deprived them, by murdering the people on whom he also obtruded them."[23] Carl Becker sees Congress's removal of this section to be a literary improvement as well as a tactical one.[24] This section might have been attacked for its logic (criticizing the king for both imprisoning slaves and freeing them), but it was too much for the shaky coalition of slave and free colonies to undertake so early. Jefferson was hoping, of course, to set the stage for ending the odious slave trade and then slavery itself and to condition his fellow southerners (and northern shippers, too) to such an expectation. Yet the whole subject was too embarrassing to bring up in the same document with such glorious rhetoric on the rights of man to self-government; and many of the slaveholders wanted no mention of inciting slaves to rebellion for fear of the power of suggestion. In any event, the whole antislavery paragraph was deleted and the cruel paradox of American slavery ignored.

Yet despite that Congress's lack of application of the precepts of freedom to the black men all around them,

Jefferson's words spell out with simplicity and grace the nutshell principles of the best of Western political thought. These principles, once enunciated so mellifluously, continue to work like yeast among all societies to bring about their full application to all men, in the fullness of time.

> We hold these truths to be self evident: that all men are created equal; that they are endowed by their Creator with certain inalienable rights; that among these are life, liberty and the pursuit of happiness; that to secure these rights, governments are instituted among men, deriving their just powers from the consent of the governed; that whenever any form of government becomes destructive of these ends, it is the right of the people to alter or to abolish it, and to institute new government, laying its foundation on such principles, and organizing its powers in such form, as to them shall seem most likely to effect their safety and happiness. . . .[25]

Here is a great, permanently revolutionary statement, one that continues to stand as a monitor against every tyrannical government, now and in the future. It is a fitting monument to Jefferson, the tireless advocate of freedom.

Notice the dynamic potential in the little word *any* in the clause, "that whenever *any* form of government becomes destructive of these ends" [italics added.] By just such a word is the principle of government for the governed *as they may decide* affirmed at *any* level, in any institution or organization. Lincoln said of this essentially literary achievement:

> All honor to Jefferson—to the man who, in the concrete pressure of a struggle for national independence by a single people, had the coolness, forecast, and capacity to introduce into a merely revolutionary document, an abstract truth, applicable to all men and all times, and so to embalm it there, that today, and in all coming days, it

shall be a rebuke and a stumbling block to the very har-
bingers of re-appearing tyranny and oppression.[26]

Jefferson himself perhaps summed up the immediate historic
effect of this American revolutionary document almost as well
in his paragraph from the *Autobiography* (1821):

> The appeal to the rights of man, which had been made in
> the United States, was taken up by France, first of the
> European nations. From her, the spirit has spread over
> those of the South. The tyrants of the North have allied
> indeed against it; but it is irresistible. Their opposition
> will only multiply its millions of human victims; their own
> satellites will catch it, and the condition of man through
> the civilized world, will be finally and greatly ameliorated.
> This is a wonderful instance of great events from small
> causes. So inscrutable is the arrangement of causes and
> consequences in this world, that a two-penny duty on tea,
> unjustly imposed in a sequestered part of it, changes the
> condition of all its inhabitants.[27]

Jefferson wrote *Notes on the State of Virginia* in 1781-1782
after retiring dispiritedly as wartime governor of the state. He
was in a fit of pique at insults to his honor concerning the
defenses of the state and the narrow escape of both the legislature and himself from British troops. Cornwallis's defeat at
Yorktown ended both the crisis in Virginia and the war, but
did little to heal Jefferson's angry renunciation of politics. It
was in recovering from this withdrawal that he threw himself
into answering a set of queries put to him earlier by a French
nobleman, Marquis de Barbe-Marbois, secretary to the
French legation in Philadelphia. The result is a hundred pages
of descriptive features of the state, plus reflections of Jefferson's views on assorted related topics. It was not at first
intended for publication, but merely to answer the Frenchman
adequately and arrange in order Jefferson's assorted mem-

oranda of conditions for his own use.[28] He published it privately in Paris in 1784 in order to have a few other copies for friends and other interested Europeans. A French edition made a marked impression in liberal circles, and it was republished in London, Germany, and America in many editions. It is reprinted, minus technical notes and tables, in Koch and Peden's *Life and Selected Writings of Thomas Jefferson* (1944), on pages 187 to 288.

Chinard calls the *Notes* "a complete conspectus of Jefferson's mind and theories at that time."[29] It includes comments on geography, wildlife, minerals, scenery, trade, political organization, scientific endeavors, slavery and its evil effects on both blacks and whites, the abilities of Negroes, Indians and their origins, and many related topics. To the modern reader, perhaps the most interesting parts are those reflecting Jefferson's early interests in science (natural history, archeology, linguistics, comparative anthropology), his progressive commitment to free public education and religious toleration, and the clues as to the real degree of acceptance of all men in the mind of this eighteenth-century aristocrat.

Science: The *Notes* contain interesting discussions calculating the origin of mammoth bones,[30] mentioning in this regard a white captive, a Mr. Stanley, taken "over the mountains west of the Missouri to a river which runs westwardly."[31] (Here is seed-thought for westward exploration which was to bear fruit with Lewis and Clark and the Oregon Territory.) After pondering what kind of animal a mammoth must be based on its widely discovered bones, Jefferson's tentative conclusion was: elephantlike but different; larger and cold-surviving. The Creator apparently has assigned the tropic zones to the elephant (as an ecological slot) and the northern or frigid zones to the mammoth (as if separate realms will separate species of similar type but different adaptability). Jefferson hypothesizes climate change (due possibly to an increase in the ecliptic angle of the earth-sun relationship) and a branching of related species to account for the difference-yet-similarity (in short, evolution); and he calculates that 250,000 years would have been required to cause that much change in climate and thus that much change in species. None of this is stated dogmatically. All hypotheses are simply suggested as possibilities open to careful scientific investigation. Many of his concepts remind the reader of Darwinism and related investigations in geology and human natural history.

According to C. W. Ceram, Jefferson's exact description and analysis of a careful excavation he made of an Indian mound (recorded in the *Notes*)[32] made him America's first scientific archeologist. In this project and description he discovered and named the basic archeological method, stratigraphy.[33] In this same passage Jefferson hypothesized likely migrations of the ancestors of the Indians across the Bering Straits (even before the lands around the Straits had been fully explored). He was not sure whether this migration went from Asia to America or the other way, but the resemblance between the east Asians and the American Indians seemed to indicate a relationship. He advocated intense linguistic study of the Indians to discover relationships and migrations, and he lamented that so many tribes had already been destroyed before this had been accomplished. Lewis and Clark, on Jefferson's instructions, were later to do as much of this as they could along with their other significant duties—exploring, surviving, mapping, making friends with Indians, and noting climate, flora, fauna, water routes, drainage and minerals. From the great number of "radical languages" among the Indians (by which Jefferson meant languages radically different from others known) he concluded that American Indian separations into tribal societies must have occurred much farther back in time than European or Old World separations. He was proposing many sensible hypotheses and fields for study from meagre information.

Government: In dealing with the government of Virginia, Jefferson gives a good history, evolution, and description; yet when he starts detailing the defects of the present (1776)

78

constitution of Virginia,[34] the writing is good for a time, but becomes rather laborious. Yet how American it is to present a detailed list of reforms to the Constitution just seven years after its adoption! Since their beginnings, Americans have traditionally sought better ways to do things based on experience rather than accept past or present methods as correct and unchangeable. Commitment to improvement is in fact the basic trait and dynamic engine of American society. And Jefferson had no small part in the strengthening of this tradition.

Negroes: There is much interesting discussion of the blacks in Virginia, revealing Thomas Jefferson as a benevolent but complete white racist (at that stage of his life). He was for emancipation and deportation of all blacks (to make this a free white man's country). He was truly against slavery, but he really believed the blacks were inherently inferior to the whites. To his credit, he projected his views as opinions only, subject to much further scientific study which certainly might lead to more accurate conclusions. Yet a good article could be written entitled "Racist Tom Jefferson" or "Tom Jefferson, White Supremacist," based on these revelations. Yet he also analyzed the destructive effects of slavery on the white owners.

> The whole commerce between master and slave is a perpetual exercise of the most boisterous passions, the most unremitting despotism on the one part, and degrading submissions on the other. Our children see this, and learn to imitate it. . . . The parent storms, the child looks on, catches the lineaments of wrath, puts on the same airs in the circle of smaller slaves, gives a loose to the worst of passions, and thus nursed, educated, and daily exercised in tyranny, cannot but be stamped by it with odious peculiarities. The man must be a prodigy who can retain his manners and morals undepraved by such circumstances. And with what execration should the statesman be loaded, who, permitting one half the citizens thus to

79

trample on the rights of the other, transforms those into despots, and these into enemies, destroys the morals of the one part, and the *amor patriae* of the other. For if a slave can have a country in this world, it must be any other in preference to that in which he is born to live and labor for another.[35]

In this regard, Jefferson's lifetime record on slavery should be considered: a second in the Virginia House of Burgesses to a motion to help the slaves (defeated); a clause in the Virginia constitution to prohibit any further importation of slaves (defeated); a bill in revising the laws of Virginia, freeing all slaves born after a certain date (defeated); a passage in the Declaration of Independence condemning the king for continuing to tolerate the slave trade (taken out by Congress); a clause in the *Report on Government for the Western Territory* (1784) to the Confederation Congress, prohibiting slavery in all the western territory (both north and south) after "the year 1800 of the Christian era."[36] This was defeated by a state vote of seven to six, a measure which if passed might have saved us sixty years of slavery and avoided the Civil War. After the defeat of this last measure, Jefferson said, "Thus we see the fate of millions unborn hanging on the tongue of one man, and Heaven was silent in that awful moment."[37] This basic territorial restriction on slavery, however, was adopted in the ordinance for the Northwest Territory (later the states of Illinois, Indiana, Michigan, Ohio, and Wisconsin). And there was the provision put in the Constitution (by Jefferson's close friend, James Madison, floor manager of the Convention) *allowing* for the end of the slave trade after 1808.

Jefferson also freed his slaves at his death. He and Washington may be chided for not freeing their slaves (and providing for their education, pay, and landholding) while president, to set precedents leading to the extinguishing of the horror both deplored. But both men also felt keenly the precariousness of the North-South coalition supporting the infant republic, and both felt union more important than emancipation for immediate survival. Indeed, Jefferson, in later years, soft-pedalled his emancipation efforts in order to dampen the secessionist sentiment he could already see threatening the Union. As he wrote in 1821:

Yet the day is not distant when it [the public] must bear and adopt it [emancipation], or worse will follow. Nothing is more certainly written in the book of fate than that these people are to be free.[38]

Education: In *Notes* Jefferson also outlined his basic 1781 plan for free public elementary schools in all districts, and a merit-scholarship system leading the better students to free public high schools and, after more sifting, on to free attendance at the university (at that time, William and Mary). "By this means twenty of the best geniuses will be raked from the rubbish annually."[39] The aristocrat of virtue and talent occasionally shows through.

By that part of our plan which prescribes the selection of the youths of genius from among the classes of the poor, we hope to avail the State of those talents which nature has sown as liberally among the poor as the rich, but which perish without use if not sought and cultivated.[40]

Although this liberal plan was not adopted in its entirety by the state, part of it, small districts five or six miles square, each establishing "a school for teaching reading, writing, and arithmetic,"[41] found its way into the public education features of the Northwest Ordinance of 1787 (one section per township reserved for school support). Thus one of the best laws of the Articles of Confederation government reflected three Jeffersonian ideas: provision for other states to be admitted on an equal basis; prohibition of slavery in future Midwest states; and provision for universal public education (as they understood the phrase: i.e., for all white males).

Beyond supporting the basic three years of three r's necessary to all free citizens to sustain the republic, Jefferson believed in vigorous education for all those able to absorb it, between eight and sixteen—especially in languages. The people especially must be taught, as the only safe "guardians of their own liberty." Their reading should be primarily historical.

> History, by apprizing them of the past, will enable them to judge of the future; it will avail them of the experience of other times and other nations; it will qualify them as judges of the actions and designs of men; and it will enable them to know ambition under every disguise it may assume; and knowing it, to defeat its views.[42]

For "every government degenerates when trusted to the rulers of the people alone."[43] Hence, "an amendment of our constitution must here come in aid of public education."[44] Thirty-five years later he still had the same views. He wrote Colonel Charles Yancey, "If a nation expects to be ignorant and free, in a state of civilization, it expects what never was and never will be."[45]

Architecture: On the state of architecture in Virginia, Jefferson commented in *Notes:* "The genius of architecture seems to have shed its maledictions over this land."[46] He found only four creditable buildings in the state, all in Williamsburg. Of these, two are described thus: "The college and hospital are rude, misshapen piles, which, but that they have roofs, would be taken for brick-kilns."[47]

Religious Toleration: Notes on Virginia also contains an excellent passage, the answers to Query XVII, on the advantages of religious freedom and freedom of thought. It begins by showing the firm grip the Anglican Church got on the colony beginning in the 1650's. This led to taxation to support the established church, discrimination and persecution. Yet

The legitimate powers of government extend to such acts only as are injurious to others. But it does me no injury for my neighbor to say there are twenty gods, or no God. It neither picks my pocket nor breaks my leg.[48]

"It is error alone which needs the support of government. Truth can stand by itself."[49]

Our sister States of Pennsylvania and New York, however, have long subsisted without any establishment at all. The experiment was new and doubtful when they made it. It has answered beyond conception. They flourish infinitely. Religion is well supported; of various kinds, indeed, but all good enough. . . . They do not hang more malefactors than we do. They are not more disturbed with religious dissensions. On the contrary, their harmony is unparalleled. . . . They have made the happy discovery, that the way to silence religious disputes, is to take no notice of them.[50]

No wonder this book was read avidly in Europe. It encapsulated America's major contribution to the art of government before that government was well underway.

The Virtues of Agricultural America: Jefferson, like most farmers, had a strong belief in rural virtue versus manufacturing and city evil. He believed at this stage in his life that the best morality, as well as the best economics, was to let America be the farming nation, and let Europe be the manufacturing ones.

Those who labor in the earth are the chosen people of God, if ever He had a chosen people, whose breasts He has made His peculiar deposit for substantial and genuine virtue . . . [He must not have been thinking of slaves here.] Corruption of morals in the mass of cultivators is a phenomenon of which no age nor nation has furnished

83

us a sample. . . . It is better to carry provisions and materials to workmen there [in Europe], than bring them to the provisions and materials, *and with them their manners and principles* [italics added]. . . . The mobs of great cities add just so much to the support of pure government, as sores do to the strength of the human body.[51]

The soil somehow magically transmitted virtue to those who crushed it in their hands, " . . . and, I repeat again, cultivators of the earth are the most virtuous and independent of citizens."[52] In our current crush of cities, we would find many who would agree. In fact, Leo Marx has written an entire book—*Machine in the Garden* (New York: Oxford University Press, 1964)—pointing out that this is one of the enduring myths of Western man. Not until after his embargo of U.S. trade during his second term as president—a move which almost bankrupted the United States—did Jefferson come around to admit grudgingly that the nation needed manufactures and commerce as much as it did agriculture.

Peace necessary to public good: The following is taken from Query XXII, The Public Income and Expenses?

Never was so much false arithmetic employed on any subject, as that which has been employed to persuade nations that it is their interest to go to war. Were the money which it has cost to gain, at the close of a long war, a little town, or a little territory, the right to cut wood here, or to catch fish there, expended in improving what they already possess, in making roads, opening rivers, building ports, improving the arts, and finding employment for their idle poor, it would render them much stronger, much wealthier and happier. This I hope will be our wisdom.[53]

Need anyone ask if Jefferson still speaks to us today?

A reading of *Notes on Virginia* will convince one that Jefferson never did write a whole book. It is more sensible to read Jefferson as Padover has arranged him, by subject matter rather than by chronological selections. One book of Jefferson selections, of his best passages, is all that is of interest from a literary standpoint to most readers. Thus Jefferson's artistry of form is limited to the sentence, the paragraph, the letter, the short unit, primarily the great liberating idea given life through the memorable expression, rather than in any *magnum opus*. His life indeed, and what he stood for, became his real *magnum opus*, not any book.

Notes on the State of Virginia, with the exceptions noted, is hardly an interesting or exciting book. No wonder he had to publish it himself. The form is not that chosen by the writer himself but that of the questioner, eliciting guidebook type information; hence, the result is a long encyclopedia-like set of replies. Yet Jefferson shows himself to be interested in being a writer by the length and detail lavished upon the answers to the questions of the French nobleman. Few people would write a hundred-page response to a request for information; yet Jefferson is impelled also by the motive of assembling his ideas on these subjects for his own use. And there is little doubt from his tone that he is proud of America and wants to tell the world about it, and perhaps elicit the immigration of the right kind of farmers and skilled craftsmen that the nation needs.

Jefferson's other partial book is his *Autobiography,* written in 1821 at the age of seventy-seven. In spite of occasional inaccuracies, it furnishes an interesting account of his life and times, from his birth through his return from Europe in the fall of 1789 and his assumption in March, 1790, of his duties as Washington's secretary of state.[54] Like Franklin and Adams before him, Jefferson wrote half an autobiography in his old age, omitting the most significant part of his life. The interesting parts are those showing his philosophy in rewriting the laws of Virginia to fit with republican ideals, the revelations of the learned Virginian in discovering Europe, and his eye-witness descriptions of France blundering step by step into the great revolution. There is a fine paragraph on the contentiousness of the Confederation Congress in which Jefferson served during 1783 and 1784, a paragraph which could be an admonition to any legislature today. It ends with:

... how can it be otherwise, in a body to which the people send one hundred and fifty lawyers, whose trade it is to question everything, yield nothing, and talk by the hour? That one hundred and fifty lawyers should do business together, ought not to be expected.[55]

He was particularly proud of his role in liberalizing the laws of Virginia, a three-year committee job (1776-79) in which he did the largest part (though most of the 126 bills presented were not passed into law until 1785-86 under Madison's legislative management). Jefferson saw to it that the following ideas were incorporated into the laws of Virginia:

1. The elimination of entail inheritance (i.e., estates passing unbreakably to heirs, and buyers of such lands not getting clear title but a kind of feudal lease) and its concomitant, primogeniture (oldest son getting entire estate).

2. The disestablishment of the Anglican church (a church of the rich supported by all taxpayers), providing instead for religious freedom. The latter resulted from his famous "Act for Establishing Religious Freedom" (1779, passed in the Assembly of Virginia, 1786), a brief masterpiece for freedom of thought.

3. General public education (the bill for "diffusion of knowledge among the people").

4. Trial by jury in the chancery courts.

Commager notes that by these legal reforms Jefferson and his supporters achieved—against his own class—a bloodless revolution in Old Dominion society. "It is honorable for us," Jefferson wrote, "to have produced the first legislature who had the courage to declare that the reason of man may be trusted with the formation of his own opinions."[56] In his discussions on government, Jefferson continued to coin quotable aphorisms.

But it is not by the consolidation, or concentration of powers, but by their distribution, that good government is effected. ... Were we directed from Washington when to sow, and when to reap, we should soon want bread.[57]

From the experience of his Paris years, 1784-89, Jefferson describes powerfully the lost chances for timely reforms to avoid the deathly sweep of the French Revolution—due mainly, in his view, to the greed and obstinacy of the queen and her clique of aristocratic supporters, jealous of their powers and dissipations. "I ever believed, that had there been no Queen, there would have been no revolution."[58]

One of his most dramatic involvements in this struggle was the use made of Jefferson's supper table as a place for a neutral-ground conference by LaFayette and various other revolutionary leaders.[59] They met to discuss how they must unite to prevent the aristocracy from continuing to dominate the nation, so that real reforms could be inaugurated. Yet Jefferson claims he was a silent listener on this occasion. He was also invited to assist in the drawing up of a new constitution for France (according to this memoir) by the Archbishop of Bordeaux, the head of a committee so charged. Yet Jefferson says he declined on the proper grounds that to do so would constitute too much interference in the internal affairs of the country to which he, a foreign diplomat, was assigned.[60] (Yet it is hard to believe he would pass up this chance.) Earlier in these pages he had summed up his role, that of advising moderation in keeping with his normal legislative strategy: secure what improvements you can into law now, and get the rest later, step by step.

I was much acquainted with the leading patriots of the Assembly. Being from a country which had successfully passed through a similar reformation, they were disposed to my acquaintance, and had some confidence in me. I urged, most strenuously, an immediate compromise; to secure what the government was now ready to yield, and trust to future occasions for what might still be wanting. It was well understood that the King would grant, at this time: (1) freedom of the person by habeas corpus; (2) freedom of conscience; (3) freedom of the press; (4) trial by jury; (5) a representative legislature; (6) annual meetings; (7) the origination of laws; (8) the exclusive right of taxation and appropriation; and (9) the responsibility of ministers; and with the exercise of these powers they could obtain in future, whatever might be further necessary to improve and preserve their constitution. They thought otherwise, however, and events have proved their lamentable error. For, after thirty years of war, foreign and domestic, the loss of millions of lives, the prostration of private happiness, and the foreign subjugation of their own country for a time, they have obtained no more, nor even that securely.[61]

It is impossible to assume that, had Jefferson acted, written, and spoken more forcibly upon these occasions, the French Revolution might have been effected peaceably. Yet his closeness to the great events and his swift summation of them make fascinating reading.

Jefferson virtually continued his *Autobiography* (or rather prepared raw material for the rest of it, uncompleted) in his "Anas," or Notes, frequent memos he wrote for his files concerning what was happening to him and the nation during the bitter Federalist-Republican struggles, 1791-1809. These memos, written in the heat of the struggles, he later revised to remove anything which might have been "incorrect, or doubtful, or merely personal or private."[62] Thus they form significant records, if not a complete literary work. In one memorable scene of a working dinner with Adams and

Hamilton (in Washington's absence) Jefferson characterizes the other two with this anecdote:

> After the cloth was removed, and our question agreed and dismissed, conversation began on other matters, and by some circumstance, was led to the British constitution, on which Mr. Adams observed, "purge that constitution of its corruption, and give to its popular branch equality of representation, and it would be the most perfect constitution ever devised by the wit of man." Hamilton paused and said, "purge it of its corruption, and give to its popular branch equality of representation, and it would become an *impracticable* government: as it stands at present, with all its supposed defects, it is the most perfect government which ever existed." And this was assuredly the exact line which separated the political creeds of these two gentlemen. The one was for two hereditary branches and an honest elective one; the other, for an hereditary King, with a House of Lords and Commons corrupted to his will, and standing between him and the people.[63]

This is a devastating revelation, if accurately reported. He goes on to characterize both Hamilton and Adams further, viewing Adams as a latter-day monarchist duped by the Hamiltonian federalist-monarchists into thinking the country was ready to accept hereditary monarchy. Again we can see that the events of history, the principles of government, and the dramatic clash of great personalities form an inseparable mesh.

Jefferson also wrote travel journals of his trips through southern France and Italy in 1787. In one of these he speculates on a Frenchman's theory concerning the occurrence of obviously marine shell-fossils 15,000 feet above the sea in the Alps. Jefferson does not accept the theory (spontaneous generation from the earth); he says more observations and study will be needed—since he thinks shells grow only with their animal hosts.[64]

In his interesting "Essay on the Anglo-Saxon Language" the key strength of English (and its source in Anglo-Saxon) is well stated: "Its copiousness, too, was much favored by the latitude it allowed of combining primitive words so as to produce any modification of idea desired."[65] (In this day of *soft-landings* and *earthrises* on the moon, of budgets *trending* toward *equal rights* and *space shuttles,* we can see how English—in America and worldwide—is carrying on with this dynamic Anglo-Saxon principle.) In this essay he urges joint British-American efforts to publish all existing Anglo-Saxon manuscripts, to modernize and make consistent their alphabets and spelling, so that they may be studied to clarify the real origins of English (which he claims are not Latin and Greek). He makes numerous concrete suggestions to facilitate this effort (later urged on the University of Virginia), particularly rejecting the complication of Anglo-Saxon (and by implication, English) by the forcing of Greek and Latin grammars upon it (them)—the great discovery of "modern" (twentieth century) English grammarians. "The Anglo-Saxon is really old English, little more difficult to understand than works we possess, and read, and still call English."[66]

Literary works of Jefferson's which should be read in their entirety include his "First Inaugural Address," delivered in Washington March 4, 1801. It is a humble, yet confident, well-organized message, designed to heal the political battle-wounds and inspire America with the barely tapped power of her ingenious republican-federal design. In the process he expresses, "within the narrowest compass they will bear," the basic principles of a democratic republic, "what I deem the essential principles of our government." Here again in a paragraph is an enunciation, as in the Declaration of Independence or the Bill of Rights, to stand forever as an ideal for free men, and a yardstick for measuring oppression. The speech is studded with memorable sentences: "I believe this, on the contrary, the strongest government on earth." "We are all republicans, we are all federalists." "Error of opinion may be tolerated where reason is left free to combat it." "Honest friendship with all nations, entangling alliances with none."

> Sometimes it is said that man cannot be trusted with the government of himself. Can he, then, be trusted with the government of others? Or have we found angels in the form of kings to govern him? Let history answer this question.[67]

The writer who had built a political party and won the presidency with his pen thus opened his extraordinarily successful first term of office.

Of Jefferson's vast correspondence no complete edition yet exists. (The Julian P. Boyd edition of the *Papers of Thomas Jefferson,* under preparation at Princeton since 1950, had reached eighteen volumes (and Jefferson's writings up to 1791) by 1971. Nor is the general reader likely to peruse much of this complete collection when it is all published. Yet many lesser collections of excellent representative letters exist to provide the reader with an adequate view of this great man's mind and writing talent. Perhaps the best of these are those presenting the great essay-duel with his federalist counterpart, John Adams, during their benign reconciliation years, 1812 to 1826: *Correspondence of Adams and Jefferson,* selected and edited by Paul Wilstach (1925, reissued in abridged form 1966); or the more complete volume II of Lester J. Cappon's *Adams-Jefferson Letters* (1959). Here the two old warriors for freedom, who had been friends, revolutionaries, diplomats together—and political enemies of the deepest dye as each fought for the presidency and a philosophy of life—rekindled their erstwhile friendship.[68] They wrote of history, philosophy, literature and religion, of past times and future possibilities—and discovered some areas of agreement, some otherwise. Well into their seventies and eighties, for twelve years they corresponded, as events and energy permitted—in their time, America's foremost literary men, exchanging a volume of thoughts worthy of ex-presidents.

Jefferson also exchanged searching philosophic opinions with Madison and Monroe, LaFayette and Kosciusko, Joseph Priestley and Benjamin Rush.[69] He wrote in one year more than 1200 replies to a continual flood of mail, while continuing to manage Monticello and plan for the University of Virginia. (He even invented a copying machine for making simultaneous duplicates of any such letters.)[70] These letters, when searched for memorable nuggets, provide some of the finest sentences and paragraphs in English.

The earth belongs to the living and not to the dead.[71]

It is incumbent on every generation to pay its own debts as it goes. A principle which, if acted on, would save one-half the wars of the world.[72]

There is not a crowned head in Europe, whose talents or merits would entitle him to be elected a vestryman by the people of any parish in America.[73]

The boisterous sea of liberty indeed is never without a wave.[74]

The freedom and happiness of man . . . are the sole objects of all legitimate government.[75]

I am not among those who fear the people. They, and not the rich, are our dependence for continued freedom.[76]

Jefferson even ended his life as the writer of hard-hitting epigrams by summing up the importance of his life in his terse epitaph:

Here was buried
Thomas Jefferson
Author of the Declaration of American Independence
of the Statute of Virginia for religious freedom
and Father of the University of Virginia

"And," he instructed, "not one word more."[77] Thus did Mr. Jefferson of Virginia, hard political fighter, wise and kind philosopher—in Chinard's phrase, "Apostle of Americanism" —go out requiring all future inquirers after him to look at his own succinct statement of himself as the best short biography. He had picked out, from the many roles in which his individual ability and devotion wrought great changes for good in the future of man, the three achievements of which he was most proud. Any one of these should have won him a deserving place in the hearts of his countrymen and the world. Yet here, too, was the secret great writer, controlling his material into and beyond the grave.

IV

[signature: John Quincy Adams]

John Quincy Adams
Writer Through Four Careers

There is such seduction in a library of good books that I cannot resist the temptation to luxuriate in reading; and, because I have so much to write, I count all time lost that is not spent in writing.

John Quincy Adams
Diary, May 24, 1839

John Quincy Adams of Massachusetts (1767-1848), sixth president of the United States (1825-29), has been the only son of a U.S. president to also achieve that high office. His father, John Adams, one of the founders of the American Revolution and the United States Constitution, introduced his son to European diplomacy and political struggle early by taking the boy along to Paris at age ten. Henry Steele Commager has written that John Quincy Adams had four public careers: diplomat, lawmaker, secretary of state, and president.[1] (It could be added that he excelled superlatively at the first three of these careers and failed only in the fourth, as president.) To these four remarkable careers, however, I would add a fifth, one usually overlooked in his panoply of achievements and offices: the career of an extraordinary, if specialized, man of letters.

John Quincy Adams, like his father and like Franklin, first caught the public eye with his ability to think and write. Three early sets of papers, presented in the *Columbian Centinel* (1791-93) over the pseudonyms Publicola, Marcellus, and Columbus, helped establish the young John Quincy, still in his twenties, as a sharp writer and thinker and a staunch defender of Washington. In fact, many, including Jefferson, thought these papers to be from the hand of the then vice-president, John Adams, though both father and son later denied they were anything but the independent work of the son. The Publicola papers brilliantly refuted Thomas Paine for his extremism and warmongering in *Rights of Man* (which had recently been presented for publication in America by Jefferson). Young Adams satirized Paine as the self-appointed "holy father of our political faith, and this pamphlet . . . his Papal Bull of infallible virtue." He criticized Paine on a number of points:

> This principle, that a whole nation has a right to do whatever it pleases, cannot in any sense whatever be admitted as true. The eternal and immutable laws of justice and of morality are paramount to all human legislation. The violation of those laws is certainly within the power, but it is not among the rights of nations.[2]

The Columbus group of papers stoutly defended Washington's policy of neutrality toward the French Revolution and consequent European wars, a policy long advocated and later followed by John Adams, but one that was unpopular with the budding Jeffersonian and Hamiltonian factions. Washington was pleased with the ability and wisdom of young Columbus, and after determining his identity, appointed him in 1794, at age twenty-six, as minister to Holland. Such high public trust so early was not founded entirely on writing ability and loyal support, however. At fourteen in Europe the young scholar had departed from his diplomat father to serve as secretary and interpreter to Francis Dana, American emissary to the Russian court of Catherine II in St. Petersburg. John Quincy Adams, Harvard graduate and practicing lawyer, was obviously a qualified young man to be given important work.

Throughout a long and adventurous diplomatic and political career John Quincy Adams wrote, with the flair of a literary man, hundreds of letters, speeches, and state papers of historical and biographical interest. The W. C. Ford edition of his *Writings* (1913-17), which runs to seven volumes collected out of the vast Adams family papers, is far from complete, ending with June 24, 1823, and thus not even including his presidency or later congressional period. In addition, between 1822 and 1824 Adams wrote, but did not conclude, a brief book, *Parties in the United States*, a potential classic on the subject which was not published until 1941.[3] After serving in both Madison's and Monroe's administrations (and himself completing a term as president), he wrote brief lives of Madison and Monroe. His 1821 *Report Upon Weights and Measures* is an eloquent plea for the American adoption of the metric system, a cause finally now being acted upon a century and a half later. He wrote and delivered brilliant antislavery speeches before constituents and Congress, delivered diatribes against the annexation of Texas (as a Union-splitting expansion of slavery), fought and won before the supreme court the deliverance of the black *Amistad* mutineers, and battled for eight years as an old man the "gag rule" against antislavery petitions in Congress. Yet in an earlier era he had written fervently also in favor of the "North American Union" and visualized the United States as a free nation expanding outward by purchase and voluntary association to encompass the entire continent (but, significantly, not the world). He anticipated, incidentally, that Russia would be America's next great adversary in the world arena, and he was always strong for the American nation so long as she was strong for freedom and virtue. In referring to Stephen Decatur's toast, "Our country, right or wrong," Adams wrote to his father in 1816:

My toast would be, may our country be always successful, but whether successful or otherwise always right. I disclaim as unsound all patriotism incompatible with the principles of eternal justice.[4]

Yet all the foregoing does not mention his greatest piece of writing, the amazingly frank diary that he kept throughout his incredible careers, spanning a half century of growth of the United States. This diary, as fitful and self-centered as it may sometimes be, is John Quincy Adams' most significant contribution to American letters. It forms a national treasure of historical and biographical insights, in vigorous, readable prose, revealing much about the men, the times and the nations in this great period of geographical expansion. Edited by his son, Charles Francis Adams (1874-77), *Memoirs of John Quincy Adams, Comprising Portions of His Diary from 1795 to 1848* runs to twelve volumes—and immediately tantalizes scholars with the thought: What about the other portions that dutiful son Charles decided to omit from publication? This question should be answered soon when presumably the new Butterfield edition of *all* the Adams papers is completed through John Quincy Adams; yet it is not of great moment to the general reader, who would be unlikely to survive the twelve volumes already available. Allan Nevins has done a greater service for the general reader by skillfully selecting one volume of the most interesting passages from the twelve and publishing them with excellent background material as *The Diary of John Quincy Adams, 1794-1845* (1928, 1951). To discover how rich with dramatic Americana the *Diary* is, take note of Allan Nevins's description in his introduction of the high points in the life of John Quincy Adams, which are illustrated on a day-by-day basis in the book:

No other American diarist touched life at quite so many points, over quite so long a period, as John Quincy Adams. He walked with the Czar Alexander I on the boulevards of St. Petersburg; he had audience with George III, who wanted to know if all the Adamses came from Massachusetts; he dined with Wellington; he saw Napoleon return to Paris from Elba; and he exchanged views with Mme. de Stael and Jeremy Bentham and Talleyrand. He saw George Washington receive the Creek chiefs; he dined repeatedly at the new White House with Jefferson, listening to his "staring" [tall] stories; and he lived to witness with disgust James K. Polk received to the Presidency amid the cheers of Democrats and slaveholders. He sat in the trial of Samuel Chase, and heard Aaron Burr make his farewell address; he was Senator from Massachusetts when the news of the *Chesapeake* outrage aroused Boston; and he was one of the grim band who voted against the resolution for the annexation of Texas—a resolution with which, he wrote, perished the liberties of mankind. He commented on the transcendentalism of Emerson and the novels of Bulwer; he shook the hand of Dickens; and he superintended the erection of the sculptures on the portico of the Capitol. He took an intense interest in science, laboring over his report on weights and measures till he suffered acutely from insomnia, and making it a classic of American metrology. To him more than any other American we owe the preservation of the Smithsonian bequest and the establishment of the Smithsonian Museum on a sound foundation. He taught oratory in Harvard University. He published original poetry, and versified Horace and La Fontaine; he read Bancroft and Byron; he expounded Shakespeare, and was proud when James H. Hackett circulated his disquisition on *Hamlet* in England; he appeared before the Supreme Court as counsel in the famous *Amistad* case. He was the chief author of the Monroe Doctrine.[5]

Nevins goes on to point out Adams's shortcomings as a diarist—his frequent waspishness, pedantry and lack of humor—but he credits him for the best that is in it, the vast panorama of portraits of the great and small, the intimate glimpses of history being made, the shrewd observations on life and nations, the readable revelations of the man himself. Nevins credits him in short as much for his diary, his incomparable record of a momentous half century, as for any of his other singular accomplishments.

To briefly remind the reader of those accomplishments—as well as John Quincy's incredible parallels to his father's roles thirty years earlier—here is a partial summary of those four careers.

Diplomat: Adams served at various times between 1794 and 1817 as minister to Holland, Prussia, Russia, Sweden, France and Great Britain. As such, he helped negotiate important trade treaties with several of these countries, and was perhaps the most effective of the American negotiators of the delicately arrived at Treaty of Ghent ending the War of 1812.[6] (His father had played the exact counterpart of this role in the previous war settlement with England ending the Revolution: the tough Yankee conservative, horsetrading England out of Transappalachia, the Northwest Territory *and* the Newfoundland fishing rights in the interests of durable peace and renewed trade. After the treaty in each case, the respective Adams was appointed American minister to England in a thankless period of ill-feeling between the two countries.) There were notable achievements of the American negotiators of the Treaty of Ghent: (1) convincing the British to make peace at all with no territorial concessions (since the United States had largely failed in arms, was powerless before the now-released British fleet and Wellington's armies and was within thirty days of utter bankruptcy as the negotiators met to sign); (2) retaining the United States-Canadian border west of the Great Lakes 150 miles north of where the British wanted it set, thus preventing Canadian trade down the Mississippi and leading to the ultimate acquisition of that strip of land by the United States all the way to the Pacific; and (3) retaining United States rights to fish the rich ocean banks off Labrador and Newfoundland.

Secretary of State: John Quincy Adams's greatest work was that which he accomplished in Monroe's cabinet (1817-25). According to Walter Lafeber, "John Quincy Adams continues to rank as the greatest Secretary of State in American history."[7] While being one of America's most aggressive and farseeing nationalists, he was able by skillful planning, counterplaying, and negotiations to *peacefully* (1) acquire Florida from Spain at virtually no cost to the United States; (2) design the Monroe Doctrine, asserting United States determination to prevent any further European colonization in the New World; (3) clear the Great Lakes of warships and establish an unfortified boundary between Canada and the United States running along the 49th parallel from roughly the Great Lakes to the Rockies; (4) remove all Russian claims to any part of the New World below Alaska; (5) remove Spanish claims to the West Coast north of the present Oregon-California border; and (6) agree with Britain to joint occupancy and settlement rights in present Oregon and Washington coast areas for ten years, renewable if both agreed again (which rights clearly would lead to United States ownership and occupancy, because Americans would settle west faster than the British). The latter three items resulted in one of John Quincy Adams's proudest achievements for his country: seventeen degrees of American latitude on the Pacific, consolidated finally by the Oregon treaty with Britain in 1846. Any one of these achievements would be enough to earn the man lasting fame; yet he was able to work bundles of such deeds into just the most illustrious of his five careers. Adams was quite right when he wrote his wife in 1822: "Of the public history of Mr. Monroe's administration, all that will be worth telling to posterity hitherto has been transacted through the Department of State."[8]

President: Though John Quincy Adams and the country survived his quiet administration with no disasters, it is generally conceded that he failed to lead the country to any significant new achievements (except worsening the South's condition through an increased protective tariff.)[9] Adams's failure as president was due not to lack of ability nor the lack of a great program, but to, in Lafeber's words, "his inept use of presidential power. He lacked the personal warmth that wins the hearts of voters, and his adherence to principle alienated many of his professional political supporters as well."[10] The nation was out of phase with the rational New Englander's philosophy for developing trade, manufactures and the West indirectly by government financed internal improvements (the New Deal a hundred years too soon) as opposed to the Jacksonian a-piece-of-the-West-for-everyone democracy. Adams also began his administration handicapped, as he (with fewer electoral votes than Jackson) acquired office from the House of Representatives when loser Henry Clay threw his support to Adams, whereupon Adams immediately appointed Clay secretary of state. Though no prior deal has ever been established, great cries of corruption immediately went up from the Jackson and Crawford forces, who thereupon began plotting Adams's defeat in the next election.

Adams's success as the previous secretary of state doubtless also contributed to his difficulties as president. The lack of severe international problems bearing on the United States undoubtedly weakened his support by the people, and his previous success at land acquisition (following the successful

102

acquisitions of George Washington, John Adams and Thomas Jefferson) had whetted the western appetite for the entire continent. The satisfaction of this appetite Adams was now resisting to prevent too rapid expansion and the obviously coming Civil War.

As early as 1820 Adams had seen that the Missouri Compromise, by not rooting out the basic spread-of-slavery problem, would lead to catastrophe for the Union. "The present question is a mere preamble—a title page to a great tragic volume."[11] He had had experience with *Northern* secessionists in the 1804-11 era; and he well knew the Southerners' fierce loyalties to their "twelve hundred millions of dollars in human beings"[12] would take them out of the Union regardless of the resulting Balkanization of North America. After much thought on the subject, still as early as 1820, he was writing in his diary, "If the Union is to be dissolved, slavery is precisely the question upon which it ought to break. For the present, however, this contest is laid asleep."[13]

Adams's basic plan for using government surplus revenues to develop canals, roads, and other internal improvements, thereby increasing the value of all public and private lands, was a farseeing and rational approach for the development of the West (finally adopted in part a century later with reclamation projects and developmental government spending). But it did not fit with the surge for greater public suffrage, free land, private profits, and squatters' sovereignty, which the Jacksonians favored. His attempts to consolidate the Union and prevent its disintegration occupied most of Adams's efforts in the White House.[14] In Lafeber's words:

> Few nations in history have lacked men willing to conquer; but few nations have produced statesmen who successfully preserved and assimilated the areas conquered. Adams attempted to reach this pinnacle of statemanship, and although he failed, he remains an heroic and tragic

figure whose failures are as instructive as his triumphs.[15]

Lawmaker: Adams's career as lawmaker divides itself into two parts: as senator (1802-08) and as congressman (1831 till his death in 1848). Adams served as Massachusetts state senator for one year, 1802-03, and as United States senator from Massachusetts, 1803-08, in both offices highly independent of his Federalist party. He finally broke with his party, several of whom were secessionist, to support Jefferson's purchase of Louisiana, the embargo, and resistance to British aggression against United States ships. For these moves, considered disloyal to New England maritime interests, the Massachusetts legislature, on June 3, 1808, elected his replacement nine months before Adams's term expired. Five days later, rather than continue to represent Massachusetts under such disapproval, Adams resigned.

His second, more significant career as lawmaker began, strangely enough, after he had failed as president and failed to get re-elected in his contest with Jackson in 1828. His oldest son, George Washington Adams, had just died at twenty-eight, and John Quincy was understandably feeling discouraged. Yet when he was asked to run for the Plymouth district seat in Congress (to win by a three-to-one vote), he again showed his independence and tireless devotion to republican government by being the only ex-president to serve in the House of Representatives. There for more than sixteen years he was the most distinguished, if cantankerously independent member, and he became "Old Man Eloquent" in his relentless championing of the right of constituents to present antislavery petitions to a hostile southern-dominated Congress. After an eight-year fight Adams saw Congress's "gag rule" against such petitions rescinded and was able to write in his diary, "Blessed, forever blessed, be the name of God!"[16]

Other achievements worth noting include the following: (1) In 1811 Adams was appointed by Madison to the United States Supreme Court, was approved by the Senate but declined the honor, perhaps sensing that his great work lay ahead in the field of diplomacy. (2) In 1841 Adams pleaded the case of the *Amistad* captives (African slaves who had seized their illegal slave ship and been in turn seized by the U.S. Coast Guard) before the Supreme Court of the United States. Adams won from the Taney court a complete release of these black men and girls rather than their return to their Spanish "owner" in Cuba, despite tremendous pressure by President Van Buren, Secretary of State Forsyth, and Attorney General Gilpin to get them returned to Cuba to prevent an international incident with Spain.[17] These gentlemen previously had repeatedly applied the same administrative pressure to the case while it plodded for eighteen months through the Connecticut district and circuit courts, so that Van Buren would not lose Southern and massive Northern anti-abolitionist support in his election year. (But the effort failed. Van Buren lost to Harrison in the 1840 election anyway.) "Old Man Eloquent" (and perhaps the death of one of the slaveholding judges while the case was before them) achieved a great moral victory for freedom, even in a land where millions were still bound by the horrors of chattel slavery.

Thus, John Quincy Adams, very like his father, helped solidify the Union with a long life of devoted service—diplomacy, lawmaking, political action and writing—and like his father always rose above party or petty localisms to independent action on principle. John Quincy Adams, in vision far ahead of the United States of his time, was a major shaper of the nation and its place in the world, a fitting son of John Adams.

The best way to appreciate the son as a writer is simply to read the diary as edited down to one volume by Nevins. Nevins uses the subtitle, *American Diplomacy and Political, Social, and Intellectual Life, from Washington to Polk*, to illustrate the scope and diversity of Adams's subject matter. Another excellent source of Adams's best selections is the latter half of

Adrienne Koch and William Peden's *Selected Writings of John and John Quincy Adams* (New York, 1946), referred to in chapter two. Most of the examples used here to show his bright writing talent are found in these volumes.

Samples may be taken chronologically (to show the evolution of his mind and times), or by subjects and personalities, or simply by dramatic interest in the man's own adventures in history and statecraft. Let us look at a few of Adams's passages on important subjects of the day, and then at some exemplary passages on personalities, to show his power with the quick sketch and incisive phrase.

Advocating North American Union (or, as Lafeber calls it, "American Continental Empire"): " . . . And by my country I mean the whole North American Union."[18] " . . . the indissoluble union of the North American continent."[19] " . . . a nation, coextensive with the North American continent, destined by God and nature to be the most populous and most powerful people ever combined under one social compact."[20]

> The whole continent of North America appears to be destined by Divine Providence to be peopled by one nation, speaking one language, professing one general system of religious and political principles. . . . I believe it indispensable that they should be associated in one federal Union.[21]

Here is manifest destiny before the phrase was coined—a common idea from Franklin and Jefferson on down, but one well expressed in word and deed by John Quincy Adams. Yet Adams was for a unified continent in order to have effective government and freedom, not dominion per se. His letter to Richard Anderson, newly appointed minister to Colombia, in 1823, shows this, in referring to Gran Colombia's (Bolivar's) ambitions for a multicontinental dominion, presumably to be made by fusing North and South America and then the world.

And the part of man, so gifted and endowed, is to enjoy, and to communicate the bounties of providence so largely lavished upon him; and not to fancy himself destined to the *empire* of the human family.[22]

Adams had seen enough of Napoleon's calamities (he had been in Russia when Napoleon invaded) not to be ambitious for any world conquest; but he was ambitious for a peaceful, voluntary, large-scale, self-governing association of men, strong enough in power and organization to protect itself in a world of ravening wolves. He felt this could only occur among virtuous, enlightened people (of which he felt there were, alas, far too few) who had skillfully designed and diligently built up sound institutions.

Slavery: Although Adams resisted being associated with the abolitionists (to avoid an extremist label fatal to his seat in Congress), there is no doubt that he hated the "peculiar institution" and saw it as the rock upon which the Union must founder unless somehow peaceful emancipation could be effected. An example of his eloquence and passion against this evil appears in his July 4, 1843, message to the people of Bangor, Maine, who were commemorating not only American independence, but Britain's peaceful, compensated emancipation in the West Indies.

The extinction of SLAVERY from the face of the earth is a problem, moral, political, religious, which at this moment rocks the foundations of human society throughout the regions of civilized man. It is indeed nothing more nor less than the consummation of the Christian religion. It is only as *immortal* beings that all mankind can in any sense be said to be born equal; and when the Declaration of Independence affirms as a self-evident truth that all men are born equal, it is precisely the same as if the affirmation had been that all men are born with immortal souls; for, take away from man his soul, the immortal spirit that is within him, and he would be a mere tameable beast of the field, and, like others of his kind, would become the property of his tamer. Hence it is, too, that, by the law of nature and of God, man can never be made the property of man. And herein consists the fallacy with which the holders of slaves often delude themselves, by assuming that the test of property is human law. The soul of one man cannot by human law be made the property of another. The owner of a slave is the owner of a living corpse; but he is not the owner of a man.[23]

Adams's many attacks on slavery over the years included a speech on April 14, 1842, foreshadowing Lincoln's emancipation proclamation: He declared that in time of war the military authority temporarily takes the place of all civil institutions.

Under this state of things, so far from its being true that the States where slavery exists have the exclusive management of the subject, not only the President of the United States but the commander of the army has power to order the universal emancipation of the slaves.[24]

Here was a man who could think, see ahead, and write so that others could understand what he saw.

Nullification (or a state asserting the right to abrogate any law of the Union): Adams's antipathy to South Carolina's advocacy of nullification (and to Texas's entry into the Union) was caused by his ardent belief in a strong national government as well as his abhorrence of slavery. The following is from his "Address to his Constituents," September 17, 1842:

Nullification was generated in the hot-bed of slavery. It drew its first breath in the land where the meaning of the word democracy is that a majority of the people are the goods and chattels of the minority; that more than

108

one-half of the people are not men, women, and children, but things, to be treated by their owners, not exactly like dogs and horses, but like tables, chairs, and joint-stools. . . . Democracy is self-government of the community by the conjoint will of the majority of members. What communion, what affinity, can there be between that principle and nullification, which is the despotism of a corporation—unlimited, unrestrained, *sovereign* power? Never, never was amalgamation so preposterous and absurd as that of nullification and democracy.[25]

This entire address abounds with vigorous, clear writing of this quality.

Admission of Texas: From the diary, December 24, 1836, comes a representative view, with typical Adams vigor:

[General James] Hamilton's report was published in the *Telegraph* of last evening. It represents the Texans as a people struggling for their liberty, and therefore entitled to our sympathy. The fact is directly the reverse—they are fighting for the establishment and perpetuation of slavery, and that is the cause of the South Carolinian sympathy with them. Can this fact be demonstrated to the understanding, and duly exhibited to the sentiment, of my countrymen? with candor, with calmness, with moderation, and with a pencil of phosphoric light? Alas, no![26]

Here is a writer, struggling with the problems of his day—and presenting an insight into one source of the Texas nationalism still evident today.

Parties in the United States: This is the title of one of Adams's clearest and most extensive works, though he apparently did not finish it to his own satisfaction and it remained unpublished until Greenberg put it out in New York in 1941. In some of Adams's most rapidly running prose, the reader receives a swift, accurate explanation of the early United States Confederation and Federation periods and their problems: what was done; what the United States under the Constitution actually became ("a national government complicated with a federation."[27] in Adams's view); what good the Federalists (who were actually the nationalists) did and why they fell. John Quincy Adams's writing here shows no partiality to John Adams, either, though of course he is partial. The sample presented includes a typical Adams swift-sketch of Hamilton, notable for its brevity, articulateness and historical accuracy, granting a trace of natural Adams bias against Hamilton.

The Alien and Sedition Laws [which J. Q. Adams elsewhere stated were "in no wise necessary"] were two engines which the Federalists borrowed from the British government and put into the hands of their adversaries to be used with extraordinary power and efficiency against themselves and against the administration. The army was the first decisive symptom of a schism in the Federal Party itself; which accomplished its final overthrow and that of the administration. The army was the creature of Colonel Hamilton and was, together with a French war, the basis of his views of personal ambition. His influence over General Washington and over the whole Federal Party was very great. His services to that cause had been eminent, his career as Secretary of the Treasury brilliant and rivalizing with that of Mr. Jefferson as Secretary of State. His talents were of the highest order, his ambition transcendent, and his disposition to intrigue irrepressible.

His consciousness of talent was greater than its reality, and, having served with reputation in the army and been for a short time an aide-de-camp of General Washington, he had convinced himself that his genius was peculiarly military and that the theatre of glory for him was at the head of an army. Perhaps this opinion was correct; great talents are of universal application. His valor was deliberate and undaunted; his experience in war not inconsiderable; the powers and resources of his mind extraordinary; his eloquence, both of speaking and writing, in the very first style of excellence; he had within him to a great degree that which subdues the minds of other men, perhaps the first of all qualities for the commander of an army. But he was of that class of characters which cannot bear a rival—haughty, overbearing, jealous, bitter and violent in his personal enmities, and little scrupulous of the means which he used against those who stood in the way of his ambition.[28]

Clearly here is a literary artist at work, one who is also an excellent historian. However, he was not always this effective.

Government financed internal improvements: Though Adams had an unassailable plan here, one which would have moderated much of the land fraud and resource devastation of the next century, his eloquence was not sufficient to sell his program to the restless, westering nation. His "First Annual Address to Congress" (State of the Union), December 6, 1825, made a brave attempt to evoke the values of a large-scale government sponsored development of the nation's heritage in lands, waters, minerals and forests. However, he just did not write well enough on this occasion (lacking perhaps the audacity to propose the whole package as did Hamilton when he presented his program for funding the state and national debts in 1791.) Yet Adams could have done a better job of selling this great idea by writing better here, by skipping the easily ridiculed astronomical observatories in favor of the more readily understandable benefits of likely inventions, great pictures of future roads, cities, states, canals, seaports on the Pacific, India trade, tunnels through mountains, bridges, mountains of wheat and corn (and schools, colleges, culture and art that would follow) clearly foreseeable and foreseen by him—yet not adequately pictured. It would have been the time to institute the relatively taxless society based on retaining the land-value growth of the developing nation as a public trust. But he did not write as vividly as usual. No wonder the people and the Congress did not accept it. And so the nation's development policies continued to congeal in forms which elevated private profit above public good.

An example of Adams's ability in satire might be the passage in his diary on *How to become president of the United States.*

[January 1, 1840] . . . A very curious philosophical history of parties might be made by giving a catalogue raisonné of the candidates for the Presidency voted for in the Electoral Colleges since the establishment of the Constitution of the United States. . . . Would not the retrospect furnish as practical principles in the operation of the Constitution—1, that the direct and infallible path to the Presidency is military service coupled with demagogue policy; 2, that in the absence of military service, demagogue policy is the first and most indispensable element of success, and the art of party drilling is the second; 3, that the drill consists in combining the Southern interest in domestic slavery with the Northern riotous Democracy; 4, that this policy and drill, first organized by Thomas Jefferson, first accomplished his election, and established the Virginia dynasty of twenty-four years, a perpetual political contradiction of his own principles; 5, that the same policy and drill, invigorated by success and fortified by experience, has now placed Martin Van Buren in the Presidential chair, and disclosed to the unprincipled ambition of the North the art of rising upon the principles of the South?[29]

Here is a master essayist, slipping hard gemstones of analysis, reflection and wit—not without bitterness, cynicism and echoes of his own personal loss—into the daily private account of his mind. He is no doubt anticipating posterity for his audience, but he is writing here, with no present audience to attack or admire.

Other subjects treated could be labeled as follows:

On the convention system:

[May 6, 1840] The members of the Baltimore Whig Convention of young men are flocking to this city by hundreds. The Convention itself consisted of thousands; an immense unwieldly mass of political machinery to accomplish nothing—to form a procession polluted by a foul and unpunished murder of one of their own marshals, and by the loss of several other lives. I am assured that the number of delegates in attendance from the single State of Massachusetts was not less than twelve hundred. And in the midst of this throng, Henry Clay, Daniel Webster, William C. Preston, Senators of the United States, and four times the number of members of the House of Representatives, have been two days straining their lungs and cracking their voices, to fill this multitude with windy sound for the glorification of William Henry Harrison and the vituperation of Martin Van Buren.[30]

If the names were changed, it could be a fair critique of many a convention since.

On the disgrace of the Lovejoy riot:

[November 22, 1837] ... The most atrocious case of rioting which ever disgraced this country happened on the night of the 7th of this month at Alton, in the State of Illinois, where a man by the name of Lovejoy, one of the leading abolitionists of the time, has been striving to establish a newspaper. Three times he had imported printing presses in the place, and three times they had

113

been destroyed by mobs, and once or twice the offices in which they were placed. The fourth time the press was imported and deposited in a merchant's warehouse. The mob assembled in the night, surrounded the warehouse, and demanded that the press should be delivered up to them. It was refused. They assailed the house with musketry, forced their way into it, set fire to the roof of the building, shot Lovejoy dead, wounded several others, till the press was delivered up to them, which they broke in pieces and threw into the river. One of the assailants also, by the name of Bishop, was killed in the affray.

This Lovejoy wrote me a letter last January, which I answered in April. He was a man of strong religious, conscientious feeling, deeply indignant at what he deemed the vices and crimes of the age. Such men are often fated to be martyrs; and he has fallen a martyr to the cause of human freedom.[31]

Thus did John Quincy Adams express his involvement and concern with the same event which inspired young Abe Lincoln to write his "Speech to the Young Men's Lyceum" against civil disobedience and violence. Students of writing might note the swift compression of Adams's reporting as well as his ability to see the significance of the event, separate report from comment, and evoke the reader's emotion through the successful, understated conveyance of his own.

No less interesting than his views and style are the hundreds of glimpses of persons great and small that people his narrative. The following are examples of his characterization.

[February 1, 1806] Mr. Baldwin made one of his serpentine speeches in favor of a temporizing policy.[32]

[April 23, 1840]... The House then went into committee of the whole on the state of the Union upon the Appropriation bill; and McKay, who had taken the floor last evening, made one of his insidious, snake-like speeches, interweaving with an ostensible defence of the present Administration venomous insinuations against me and mine. McKay is a political Mrs. Candour, smooth as oil in outward form and fetid as a polecat in inward savor. He damned with faint praise my report of the minority of the Committee on Manufactures in February, 1833. I made no answer; but Evans, of Maine, gave him an instantaneous and most effectual threshing, which left his argument not a whole bone.[33]

John Marshall (loyal to the wily old Federalist):

[February 13, 1831] Wirt spoke to me also in deep concern and alarm at the state of Chief-Justice [John] Marshall's health. . . . His mind remains unimpaired, but his body is breaking down. He has been thirty years Chief Justice of the Supreme Court, and has done more to establish the Constitution of the United States on sound construction than any other man living. The terror is, that if he should be now withdrawn some shallow-pated wild-cat like Phillip P. Barbour, fit for nothing but to tear the Union to rags and tatters, would be appointed in his place.[34]

Emerson:

[August 2, 1840] . . . A young man, named Ralph Waldo Emerson, and a classmate of my lamented son George, after failing in the everyday avocations of a Unitarian preacher and schoolmaster, starts a new doctrine of transcendentalism, declares all the old revelations super-annuated and worn out, and announces the approach of new revelations and prophecies. . . . Mr. Lunt's discourse this morning was intended to counteract the effect of these wild and visionary phantasies, and he spoke with just severity of the application of this spirit of hurly-burly innovation to the most important and solemn duties of the Christian faith.[35]

Emerson a year earlier had said of Adams:

. . . a man of audacious independence that always kept the public curiosity alive in regard to what he might do. . . . A bruiser . . . who cannot live on slops but must have sulphuric acid in his tea.[36]

Van Buren:

[April 13, 1836] Van Buren, like the Sosie of Moliere's *Amphitryon,* is "l'ami de tout le monde." This is perhaps the great secret of his success in public life, and especially against the competitors with whom he is now struggling for the last step on the ladder of his ambition—Henry Clay and John C. Calhoun. They indeed are left upon the field for dead; and men of straw, Hugh L. White, William H. Harrison, and Daniel Webster, are thrust forward in their places.[37]

[December 5, 1837] The House at noon was called to order . . . Van Buren's message gave me a fit of melancholy for the future fortunes of the republic. Cunning and duplicity pervade every line of it. The sacrifice of the rights of Northern freedom to slavery and the South, and the purchase of the West by the plunder of the public lands, is the combined system which it discloses. It is the system of Jackson's message of December, 1832, covered with a new coat of varnish.[38]

[September 9, 1837] I called at the President's house, and spent half an hour in conversation with him respecting the weather, the climate, and Queen Victoria, the girl of eighteen, sovereign of all the British dominions—

"Youth at the prow, and Pleasure at the helm."

... There are many features in the character of Mr. Van Buren strongly resembling that of Mr. Madison—his calmness, his gentleness of manner, his discretion, his easy and conciliatory temper. But Madison had none of his obsequiousness, his sycophancy, his profound dissimulation and duplicity. In the last of these he much more resembles Jefferson, though with very little of his genius. The most disgusting part of his character, his fawning servility, belonged neither to Jefferson nor to Madison.[39]

Reflecting the smart of old wounds, Adams yet writes with vividness on a panoply of leaders.

Calhoun:

[October 10, 1837]... The Divorce or Sub-Treasury bill from the Senate was called up... by Pickens, of South Carolina, who made in support of it a prepared speech of two hours, with which he has been swelling like a cock turkey ever since Calhoun's bargain and sale of himself to Van Buren, at the commencement of this session. Pickens is a fixture to the house of Calhoun, and Van Buren bought him with Calhoun.[40]

Aaron Burr:

[November 5, 1804]... The Vice-President Mr. Burr, on the 11th of July last fought a duel with General Alexander Hamilton, and mortally wounded him, of which he died the next day. The coroner's inquest on his body found a verdict of wilful murder by Aaron Burr, Vice-President of the United States. The Grand Jury in the County of New York found an indictment against him, under the statute, for sending the challenge; and the Grand Jury of Bergen County, New Jersey, where the duel was fought, have recently found a bill against him for murder. Under all these circumstances Mr. Burr appears and takes his seat as President of the Senate of the United States.[41]

[November 16, 1837, on reading Matthew L. Davis's *Life of Aaron Burr*]... He lived and died as a man of the world—brave, generous, hospitable, and courteous, but ambitious, rapacious, faithless and intriguing. This character raised him within a hair's breadth of the Presidency of the United States, sunk him within a hair's breadth of a gibbet and halter for treason, and left him, for the last thirty years of his life, a blasted monument of Shakespeare's vaulting ambition.[42]

[December 6, 1837]... The failure of my father's re-election in 1801 was the joint work of Burr and Alexander Hamilton; and it is among the most remarkable examples of Divine retributive justice, that the result to them was the murder of one of them in a duel, and the irretrievable ruin of the murderer by the very accomplishment of his intrigues. Even-handed justice never held a better balance scale.[43]

Though eloquent and essentially true, this is perhaps quite unfair to Hamilton, who apparently helped break the electoral tie in 1801, giving the presidency to his hated rival Jefferson in preference to surrendering the country to Burr or to the anarchy of no legal succession. For in any event, John Adams had not polled enough votes.

Jefferson: As a young senator, Adams had of course known President Thomas Jefferson, come to support him, and repeatedly dined in the glow of presidential affability. But as he worked at writing his Madison eulogy in 1836, Adams researched Madison and Jefferson anew through the posthumously published correspondence of Jefferson and wrote the following:

[August 29, 1836]... It shows his craft and duplicity in very glaring colors. I incline to the opinion that he was not altogether conscious of his own insincerity, and deceived himself as well as others. His success through a long life, and especially from his entrance upon the office of Secretary of State under Washington until he reached the Presidential chair, seems, to my imperfect vision, a slur upon the moral government of the world. His rivalry with Hamilton was unprincipled on both sides. His treatment of my father was double-dealing, treacherous, and false beyond all toleration. His letter to Mazzei, and his subsequent explanations of it, and apologies for it, show that he treated Washington, as far as he dared, no better than he did my father; but it was Washington's popularity that he never dared to encounter. His correspondence now published proves how he dreaded and detested it. His letter to my father, at the first competition between them for the Presidency, the fawning dissimulation of his first address as Vice-President to the Senate, with his secret machinations against him from that day forth, show a character in no wise amiable or fair; but his attachment to those of his friends whom he could make useful to himself was thoroughgoing and exemplary. Madison moderated some of his excesses, and refrained from following others. He was in truth a greater and a far more estimable man.[44]

Here is a writer who, for all his evident bias, can present a swift, understandable character analysis. The words have perfectly become the tools of the mind. Adams continues on Jefferson in his next day's entry (August 30, 1836):

I wrote little, and continued reading the letters of Jefferson from 1793 till August, 1803, published by his grandson. His duplicity sinks deeper and deeper into my mind. His hatred of Hamilton was unbounded; of John Marshall, most intense; of my father, tempered with compunctious visitings, always controlled by his ambition. They had been cordial friends and cooperators on the great cause of independence, and as joint Commissioners abroad after the Peace of 1783; there had then been a warm and confidential intimacy between them, which he never entirely shook off, but which he sacrificed always to his ambition, and, at the last stage of his life, to his envy and his poverty; for he died insolvent, and on the very day of his death received eleemosynary donations from the charity of some of those whom he had most deeply injured. This circumstance is not creditable to his country. She ought not to have suffered a man, who had served her as he had, to die with his household wanting the necessaries of life. But it was the natural consequence of the niggardly doctrines which his political system had imposed upon him, and which he had passed off upon the country for patriotism. . . . I am compelled to draw many other harsh conclusions against this great man from his now published letters.[45]

Napoleon in Russia: Adams wrote the following in a letter to his brother, T. B. Adams, from St. Petersburg, November 24, 1812:

. . . The empire of Napoleon was built upon victory alone. Defeat takes away its foundations, and with such defeat as he is now suffering it would be nothing surprising to see the whole fabric [previously called "the Colossus of French power"] crumble into ruins. France, indeed, still remains a formidable mass of power, but into what condition she may be plunged by the overthrow of his government I am scarcely able to conjecture. The day of trial in Russia has been severe, but it has been short, and her deportment under it will raise her high in the estimation of mankind. Her plan of defence has the most decisive demonstration in its favor—success—and success under numerous incidental circumstances disadvantageous to her. Not only her armies, but her peasantry, armed and sent into the field as if by enchantment, have fought with the most invincible courage, though not always with favorable fortune. The chances of war have been sometimes with and sometimes against them, but they have arrested the career of the conqueror of the age, and drawn him on to ruin, even when they have yielded him the victory.[46]

John Quincy Adams, who at forty-five in his "honorable exile" in Russia lamented that he had not yet done anything significant for "my country or . . . mankind," certainly never gave up trying. As the most illustrious member of the House of Representatives in his later years, as champion of the right of constituents to petition and of slaves to be free, he became a rallying center, if not for the whole abolition movement, at least for the moderate progressives who wanted a non-land-grabbing government—those who wanted justice to be done and slavery to be extinguished without rending the Union. During the thirties and forties, the breach between North and South was widening, and passions on the issue of slavery versus freedom were hardening into rage. The over-ocean slave trade, though illegal for most nations, was still thriving through smuggling—causing thousands to die for the enrichment of the few. The slave states' interstate trade in human flesh was steadily rending families and crushing human lives. To close our sketch of Adams's writing, here is his diary entry of March 29, 1841, showing the difficulties of the role he had chosen to play in his seventies. He presages here the final "gag rule" victory of 1844 and the anguish of the victory of the Union itself over removing the great cancer of slavery from within its heart.

I am yet to revise for publication my argument in the case

of the *Amistad* Africans; and, in merely glancing over the slave-trade papers lent me by Mr. Fox, I find impulses of duty upon my conscience which I cannot resist, while on the other hand are the magnitude, the danger, the insurmountable burden of labor to be encountered in the undertaking to touch upon the slave-trade. No one else will undertake it; no one but a spirit unconquerable by man, woman or fiend can undertake it but with the heart of martyrdom. The world, the flesh, and all the devils in hell are arrayed against any man who now in this North American Union shall dare to join the standard of Almighty God to put down the African slave-trade; and what can I, upon the verge of my seventy-fourth birthday, with a shaking hand, a darkening eye, a drowsy brain, and with all my faculties dropping from me one by one, as the teeth are dropping from my head— what can I do for the cause of God and man, for the progress of human emancipation, for the suppression of the African slave-trade? Yet my conscience presses me on; let me but die upon the breach.[47]

Seven years later, he did just that. In the House of Representatives, shortly after voting "No" on a resolution to award medals to American officers who fought in the Mexican War, John Quincy Adams, while writing diligently at his desk, suffered a stroke. Two days later he was dead.

The writing he leaves behind is valuable for many reasons: the eloquence of his style, the glimpses of dramatic history, the insights of his mind, the range and variety of experience in a long, illustrious life. But perhaps its most fascinating quality is its continuous reflection of the merit and character of John Quincy Adams himself.

V

Abraham Lincoln

Lincoln's Literary Achievement

In some of the most moving prose ever written, Lincoln rededicated the American nation to the advancement of human liberty and thus gave universal meaning to a domestic conflict. This was his great literary achievement.[1]

Don E. Fehrenbacher

Because of the importance of his ideas, the decisive location of Lincoln in history, and the immense drama of his personal life, Lincoln as a major literary figure is often overlooked even by his most admiring biographers. Roy Basler, able editor of _Abraham Lincoln: His Speeches and Writings_ (1946) and

Note: Where the author judges that conventionally placed footnote numbers interfere with the esthetic effect of passages quoted for esthetic effect, he has placed those numbers earlier in the description of those passages. He has also corrected Lincoln's spelling, if necessary, to avoid the use of _sic_.

Collected Works (1953-55), writes in his perceptive introduction to the former, "Lincoln's Development as a Writer": "As literary critics, Lincoln's biographers have displayed, with few exceptions, a lack of literary perspective exceeded only by their preoccupation with political facts."[2] For example, Allan Nevins in "Lincoln in his Writings,"—the introduction to Philip Stern's *Life and Writings of Abraham Lincoln* (1940), sees Lincoln's writings as primarily of interests historical and biographical, and of some smaller literary interest in his latest and best work—"but that actually belongs to the study of the man, *for he never deliberately tried to be a literary artist* [italics added], and wrote only to express his thought and emotions."[3] Nevins thus patently misses the reality of Lincoln's creative genius with words, his intentional self-aware construction of esthetic effect in his medium for increased emotional and intellectual impact on the reader or listener. True, Lincoln was always trying to reach the listener or reader with his logic, point of view, program, or idea; yet there was always a conscious savor for the power and ring of phrase and sentence, a devotion to an overall design and strategy, as well as the tact of a master diplomat and judge of men. His basic operative policy seemed to be: "If I were in his shoes, what would persuade me?" Certainly not bombast, falsehoods, easy promises, arrogant didacticism or condescension—and least of all threats, vengeance and force. Humor, anecdotes, reasons, vivid metaphor, simplicity, brevity, biblical and Shakespearean rhythms, and sincere appeals to the ideals of democracy (freedom for all men, union of the United States of America, moderation, forgiveness, the moral horror of slavery, and the cynical abuse of these ideals by the perpetrators of slavery)—all these were Abraham Lincoln's stock in trade as a thinker-doer-writer, the greatest of his age. The fact that he was not a writer of *belles lettres,* poems, novels or plays makes him no less a literary artist.

He did make a few efforts to write poetry as a young man, notably those written in 1846 upon revisiting his boyhood home in Indiana. Two of his more respectable efforts, "My Childhood Home Again I See" and "The Bear Hunt," are included in Basler's single volume of selections. The former, a touching poem, ends with this creditable stanza.[4]

> The very spot where grew the bread
> That formed my bones, I see.
> How strange, old field, on thee to tread
> And feel I'm part of thee!

The fact that he cast the last line as he did (instead of "And feel you're part of me!") is an early evidence of the size of his character, of his ability to look at himself and others with detachment and unselfishness.

Earlier, in August, 1842, he had ventured into satirical fiction in writing the second of a series of pseudonymous "Letters from the Lost Townships" to the Sangamo *Journal*.[5] This piece, though on a political subject (the cancelling of the State acceptance of State Bank paper for taxes), shows a humorous story-telling talent on a par with that of Mark Twain at the same age. The piece is cast as a letter to the printer from Rebecca, the aunt of Jeff and Peggy, neighborly characters who bring out the meaning of the attack through dialog. It reveals imagination, skillful characterization, humor very much like Twain's, a blistering satirical attack on State Auditor James A. Shields, skill with dialect-dialog, vivid imagery, and Lincoln's usual clarity and brevity. A sample passage follows.[6]

They had a sort of a gatherin there one night, among the grandees, they called a fair. All the galls about town was there, and all the handsome widows, and married women, finickin about, trying to look like galls, tied as tight in the middle, and puffed out at both ends like bundles of fodder that hadn't been stacked yet, but wanted stackin pretty bad. And then they had tables all round the house kivered over with baby caps, and pin-cushions, and ten thousand such little nick-nacks, tryin to sell 'em to the fellows that were bowin, and scrapin and kungeerin about 'em. They wouldn't let no democrats in, for fear they'd disgust the ladies, or scare the little galls, or dirty the floor. I looked in at the window, and there was this same fellow Shields floatin about on the air, without heft or earthly substance, just like a lock of cat-fur where cats had been fightin.

Perhaps fortunately, this effort led not to acclaim and profit as a writer (as it very well might have under other circumstances) but to a challenge to a duel by Shields and very nearly to the consummation of such a tragedy. They got as far as drawing up the rules of the duel before Lincoln apologized enough to avoid the fray. Had the affair led to a happy outcome, Lincoln might have been launched on a purely literary career rather than a political-literary one.

Basler, after reviewing Lincoln's youthful efforts in poetry and satire, finds him (as Chinard found John Adams) guided by the limitations of his writing environment more and more into the legal and political arenas.

In Lincoln we have a literary artist, constrained by social and economic circumstances and a dominant political tradition to deal with facts as fact, yet always motivated by his love of words and symbols and his eternal craving to entertain people and to create beauty. It is this love of words, never completely subservient, which finally flowers in the unique art of his "Gettysburg Address," "Farewell Address," "Second Inaugural Address,"

... Lincoln spoke as an artist because he was first of all an artist at heart. Had he otherwise developed these talents, it is not difficult to imagine for him an important place among American poets or writers of fiction.[7]

128

Jacques Barzun in *Lincoln, the Literary Genius* (1960) sees the unrecognized literary artist as the one facet of Lincoln—different from his several legends—which the later reader can rediscover for himself. Barzun chides previous biographers and historians for not being sufficient literary critics to discern what Lincoln had in literary ability and note how it developed. Barzun finds

> inadequate criticism, overfamiliarity with a few specially notable examples of Lincoln's writing, ignorance of his early work, and the consequent suppression of one whole side of his character. . . .[8]

> . . . wording his thoughts with complete clarity, while adapting their order and form to what he surmised others must be thinking. . . . He had, in short, the secret of infallible exposition . . . order first, and then a lightning-like brevity.[9]

Barzun illustrates this fierce, intentional economy thus:

> Here is how he writes in 1846, a young politician far from the limelight, and of whom no one expected a lapidary style: "If I falsify in this you can convict me. The witnesses live, and can tell." There is in this challenge a fire and a control which show the master. And yet the occasion was commonplace, like many other incidents of life about which Lincoln wrote innumerable sentences of equal vividness and force.[10]

A later example of this passion for brevity-yet-completeness is Lincoln's response to an alleged peace feeler urged on him by Horace Greeley in 1864.[11]

> Any proposition which embraces the restoration of peace, the integrity of the whole Union, and the abandonment

of slavery, and which comes by and with an authority that can control the armies now at war against the United States will be received and considered by the executive government of the United States, and will be met by liberal terms on other substantial and collateral points; and the bearer, or bearers thereof shall have safe-conduct both ways.

Was there ever a government official who could say what he meant better than that? There is the essence of a peace treaty, as well as important details for working it out, complete in one sentence.

Again, the entire "Farewell Address at Springfield," as Lincoln departed from his friends of half a lifetime to take up an ominous presidency, is but one apt paragraph.[12] Note how Lincoln uses commas as does Walt Whitman, to build a prose poem of psalmlike rhythms, to convey the dignity of the occasion and express his real feelings of sadness and life-passing, yet responsibility and gratitude at this sad parting.

My Friends:
No one, not in my situation, can appreciate my feeling of sadness at this parting. To this place, and the kindness of these people, I owe everything. Here I have lived a quarter of a century, and have passed from a young to an old man. Here my children have been born, and one is buried. I now leave, not knowing when or whether ever I may return, with a task before me greater than that which rested upon Washington. Without the assistance of that Divine Being who ever attended him, I cannot succeed. With that assistance, I cannot fail. Trusting in Him who can go with me, and remain with you, and be everywhere for good, let us confidently hope that all will yet be well. To His care commending you, as I hope in your prayers you will commend me, I bid you an affectionate farewell.

Even in this short a space he turns a few parting words into a benediction upon his town and homeland, upon himself in his new duties and upon the nation.

Yet brevity and emotional sincerity are only part of the power of Lincoln's art. Metaphor, parable, homely illustration, vigorous slang alternating with biblical solemnity and clear statement of profound ideas enliven his spare lines. His brief telegram of June 14, 1863, to General Joseph Hooker[13] ends with the following:

> If the head of Lee's army is at Martinsburg, and the tail of it on the Plank road between Fredericksburg and Chancellorsville, the animal must be very slim somewhere. Could you not break him?

Yet coupled with brevity and vigorous image is an entire incisiveness that clarifies the idea while it convinces the reader. A paragraph from Lincoln's letter to Joshua Speed of August 24, 1855,[14] will serve as an illustration.

> I am not a Know-Nothing. That is certain. How could I be? How can any one who abhors the oppression of the negroes, be in favor of degrading classes of white people? Our progress in degeneracy appears to me to be pretty rapid. As a nation, we began by declaring that *"all men are created equal."* We now practically read it "all men are created equal, *except negroes.*" When the Know-Nothings get control, it will read "all men are created equal, except negroes, *and foreigners, and Catholics.*" When it comes to this I should prefer emigrating to some country where they make no pretense of loving liberty— to Russia, for instance, where despotism can be taken pure, and without the base alloy of hypocrisy.

Barzun notes that clues to the artist emerge in the attractions of his style, independent of subject matter:

The pleasure it gives is that of lucidity and motion, the incredibly rapid and graceful motion of Lincoln's mind.[15]

... and by its [the paragraph's] movement, like one who leads another in the dance, it catches up our thought and swings it into eager compliance.[16]

Sandburg reports that Lincoln, in admiring the wartime humorous writing of Artemus Ward and others, remarked to Sumner, "For the genius to write these things, I would gladly give up my office."[17] And in 1846, referring to a friend's hint that he might have written "Mortality," a poem by William Knox, Lincoln wrote, "Beyond all question, I am not the author. I would give all I am worth, and go in debt, to be able to write so fine a piece as I think that is."[18]

Fehrenbacher in the introduction already cited, reiterated the idea that Lincoln's political and spiritual achievements hinged on his literary ability:

Lincoln's great accomplishment was to articulate the national purpose so convincingly and mobilize the national will so thoroughly that the Union could not be shaken by military defeats or internal discord.[19]

Thus, one-half of this great accomplishment was the thinking-writing-speaking portion of it—the articulation—essentially the literary achievement. The other half of it, of course, was providing the leadership and administrative genius, the strength of character and sustaining spiritual power necessary to effect the ideas.

Lincoln's literary talent was not always committed to high political and military purpose. His strength of spirit and devotion to morality were evident in many of the earlier passages and letters. In his modest 1850 "Notes for a Law Lecture,"[20] he wrote, among other fine passages:

Discourage litigation. Persuade your neighbors to compromise whenever you can. Point out to them how the nominal winner is often a real loser—in fees, expenses, and waste of time. As a peacemaker the lawyer has a superior opportunity of being a good man. There will still be business enough.

This was when he was out of office and with no likely prospects of ever being re-elected again—after alienating his former district over criticizing our entry into the Mexican War.

Later, as Lincoln grew to meet the demands of his presidential calling, his urge to communicate continued to range in spirit beyond mere politics or nationalism. It is this reward of universal wisdom in powerful rhythmic language (coming out of the daily struggles of the Civil War generation) which the modern reader finds so refreshing. Lincoln's "Meditation on the Divine Will," written for his own contemplation probably in September, 1862, illustrates the process and his art as well as his own religious faith. It also presages the basic idea of the "Second Inaugural Address":

The will of God prevails. In great contests each party claims to act in accordance with the will of God. Both may be, and one must be, wrong. God cannot be for and against the same thing at the same time. In the present civil war it is quite possible that God's purpose is something different from the purpose of either party; and yet the human instrumentalities, working just as they do, are of the best adaptation to effect his purpose. I am almost ready to say that this is probably true; that God wills this contest, and wills that it shall not end yet. By his mere great power on the minds of the now contestants, he could have either saved or destroyed the Union without a human contest. Yet the contest began. And, having begun, he could give the final victory to either side any day. Yet the contest proceeds.

Though John Hay tells us this "was not written to be seen of men," one may wonder how such a perfect contemplation happened to be lying where Abraham Lincoln's loyal secretary would find it.[21]

Basler sees Lincoln to be philosophically as much a romantic as Emerson, Thoreau, Whitman, Whittier, Lowell, Channing, Parker and Garrison. Like them, Lincoln believed in human perfectibility, progressive improvement through education, exaltation of reason through which progress may be achieved, ideals of liberty, equality and brotherhood—in short, the humanitarianism of Jefferson.[22] Basler sees a consistent adherence to these beliefs throughout Lincoln's works.

> It is clear in "The Perpetuation of Our Political Institutions" that the fundamental theme of the "Gettysburg Address," which was later to be woven out of these very concepts, was essentially in 1838 what it was in 1863, the central concept in Lincoln's philosophy. Lincoln thought of American democracy as an experiment in achieving human liberty, relatively successful though far from completed, and threatened most by the mobocratic spirit and the failure of the citizens to observe and preserve the duly constituted authority of government.[23]

Another trait of Lincoln's writing is his ability to render the products of massive research into swift, clear, smooth-flowing yet logical prose. Basler, citing a preface to a published version of the "Cooper Institute Address," quotes editor Charles Nott on Lincoln's ability to research and condense:

> A single, easy, simple sentence of plain Anglo-Saxon words contains a chapter of history that, in some in-

stances, has taken days of labor to verify and which must have cost the author months of investigation to acquire.[24]

Further, in a letter to Lincoln concerning its publication, Nott wrote:

> I cannot help adding that this is an extraordinary example of condensed English. After some experience in criticizing for Reviews, I find hardly anything to touch and nothing to omit. It is the only one I know of which I cannot shorten, and—like a good arch—moving one word tumbles a whole sentence down.[25]

Besides clarity and brevity, respect for the reader or the audience is a constant trait in Lincoln's writing. In a private letter to A. H. Stephens of Georgia,[26] a friend from congressional days who was soon to become vice-president of the Confederacy, Lincoln wrote December 22, 1860—fighting to turn back secession:

> Do the people of the South really entertain fears that a Republican administration would, directly, or indirectly, interfere with their slaves, or with them, about their slaves? If they do, I wish to assure you, as once a friend, and still, I hope, not an enemy, that there is no cause for such fears.

> The South would be in no more danger in this respect, than it was in the days of Washington. I suppose, however, this does not meet the case. You think slavery is *right*, and ought to be extended; while we think it is *wrong* and ought to be restricted. That I suppose is the rub. It certainly is the only substantial difference between us.

Perhaps the most all-pervasive trait in Lincoln's writing is his clear thinking. In July of 1854, Lincoln wrote out some notes to analyze the logic of slavery:[27]

> If A. can prove, however conclusively, that he may, of right, enslave B., why may not B. snatch the same argument, and prove equally that he may enslave A.?
>
> You say A. is white, and B. is black. It is color, then; the lighter, having the right to enslave the darker? Take care. By this rule, you are to be slave to the first man you meet, with fairer skin than your own.
>
> You do not mean color exactly? You mean the whites are intellectually the superiors of the blacks, and therefore have the right to enslave them? Take care again. By this rule, you are to be slave to the first man you meet, with an intellect superior to your own.
>
> But, say you, it is a question of *interest;* and, if you can make it your *interest,* you have the right to enslave another. Very well. And if he can make it his interest, he has the right to enslave you.

This was the kind of merciless reasoning and incisive language that was soon to descend upon Stephen Douglas after he pushed through Congress his Kansas-Nebraska Bill of 1854. This bill allowed the new territories of Kansas or Nebraska to have slavery north of the Missouri Compromise line of 1820, if the territorial settlers (presumably whites only) so voted. This act, seen by Lincoln and many others as the opening of a campaign to legalize slavery everywhere in the Union, aroused him anew to politics, led to the formation of the Republican Party, and gave him the issue whereby he became a national figure.

One of his many responses to this law also illustrates another strong point of Lincoln's writing—his deft use of metaphor or anecdote. On September 11, 1854, he planted an unsigned editorial in the Illinois *Journal*.[28] After clarifying the language and meaning of the new law, the tall ghost editorialist wrote:

To illustrate the case—Abraham Lincoln has a fine meadow, containing beautiful springs of water, and well fenced, which John Calhoun had agreed with Abraham (originally owning the land in common) should be his, and the agreement had been consummated in the most solemn manner, regarded by both as sacred. John Calhoun, however, in the course of time, had become owner of an extensive herd of cattle—the prairie grass had become dried up and there was no convenient water to be had. John Calhoun then looks with a longing eye on Lincoln's meadow, and goes to it and throws down the fences, and exposes it to the ravages of his starving and famishing cattle. "You rascal," says Lincoln, "what have you done? What did you do this for?" "Oh," replies Calhoun, "everything is right. I have taken down your fence; but nothing more. It is my true intent and meaning not to drive my cattle into your meadow, nor to exclude them therefrom, but to leave them perfectly free to form their own notions of the feed, and to direct their movements in their own way!"

Now would not the man who committed this outrage be deemed both a knave and a fool,—a knave in removing the restrictive fence, which he had solemnly pledged himself to sustain;—and a fool in supposing that there could be one man found in the country to believe that he had not pulled down the fence for the purpose of opening the meadow for his cattle?

Here is hard-hitting parable blended with enough Lincoln humor to make it almost a parody of the parable form.

Evidences of art appear not only in its swiftness, condensation and bold personification, but in the way extraneous words are allowed in lovingly to improve its mellifluousness and disguise its fierce rush of condensation: "consummated in the most solemn manner"; "the ravages of his starving and famishing cattle"; "my true intent and meaning"—each phrase of which in its completeness improves the overall beauty and impact of the language, in spite of the redundancy. Another evidence of the artist is his transmutation of Douglas into the more readily understandable Calhoun, a personality also more associated with the Missouri Compromise. The parable is also interesting as a secret glimpse of Lincoln's clear-cut ambition, as he cast himself, even in satire, as leader of free-state forces as early as 1854.

Yet from satire, he could turn on the same subject to other modes: a crusading appeal for justice and the American tradition (next passage), or a gentle plea on the most holy of motives (following). Both of these are within a few lines of each other in his great Peoria speech, "The Repeal of the Missouri Compromise," given on October 16, 1854.[29]

These principles [self-government and slavery] can not stand together. They are as opposite as God and mammon; and whoever holds to the one, must despise the other. When Pettit, in connection with his support of the Nebraska Bill, called the Declaration of Independence "a self-evident lie," he only did what consistency and candor require all other Nebraska men to do. Of the forty odd Nebraska Senators who sat present and heard him, no one rebuked him. Nor am I apprized that any Nebraska newspaper, or any Nebraska orator, in the whole nation, has ever yet rebuked him. If this had been said among Marion's men, Southerners though they were, what would have become of the man who said it? If this had been said to the men who captured Andre, the man who said it, would probably have been hung sooner

138

than Andre was. If it had been said in old Independence Hall, seventy-eight years ago, the very door-keeper would have throttled the man, and thrust him into the street.

Here we have the Lincolnian arts: simplicity, brevity, principles made clear, the smooth integration of researched facts, knowledge of history, and specific examples—in this case, a triple hypothetical one, each parallel scene gathering increasing force. Two equally eloquent paragraphs later he moderates into the persuasive finale.

> Our republican robe is soiled, and trailed in the dust. Let us re-purify it. Let us turn and wash it white, in the spirit, if not the blood, of the Revolution. Let us turn slavery from its claims of "moral right" back upon its existing legal rights, and its arguments of "necessity." —Let us return it to the position our fathers gave it; and there let it rest in peace. Let us re-adopt the Declaration of Independence, and with it, the practices, and policy, which harmonize with it. Let north and south—let all Americans—let all lovers of liberty everywhere—join in the great and good work. If we do this, we shall not only have saved the Union; but we shall have so saved it, as to make, and to keep it, forever worthy of saving. We shall have so saved it, that the succeeding millions of free happy people, the world over, shall rise up, and call us blessed, to the latest generations.

Note how, despite the oratorical stance and the biblical rhythms, he is very accurately assessing America's plight under slavery and her decisive role in man's worldwide cultural evolution.

For all his concern as to the moral wrong of slavery in general and the political error of letting slavery into formerly free territories, Lincoln was not an abolitionist. He was a moderate conservative of a most gradual persuasion. His constitutional amendment proposed (but not adopted) late in 1862 set the year 1900 for the completion of compensated emancipation.[30] His literary powers become evident time and again in speeches and messages aiming at preserving the Union first while letting slavery die a natural death when the states concerned would voluntarily end it. Perhaps his plainest expression of this view was his famous reply to editor Horace Greeley,[31] who had been, earlier in 1862, bitterly attacking Lincoln for not freeing all the slaves by decree.

> My paramount object in this struggle is to save the Union, and is *not* either to save or to destroy slavery. If I could save the Union without freeing *any* slave I would do it; and if I could save it by freeing *all* the slaves I would do it; and if I could save it by freeing some and leaving others alone I would also do that. What I do about slavery, and the colored race, I do because I believe it helps to save the Union; and what I forbear, I forbear because I do *not* believe it would help save the Union. . . .
>
> I have here stated my purpose according to my view of *official* duty; and I intend no modification of my oft-expressed *personal* wish that all men every where could be free.

He was fighting to retain the four slaveholding border states—Delaware, Maryland, Kentucky and Missouri—within the Union, while pleading with them to undertake their own programs of compensated emancipation since slavery had become the emotional focus of the war. His own message to Congress[32] entreating national reimbursement to states granting compensated emancipation (December 1, 1862—one month before the scheduled Emancipation Proclamation was to take effect) ended with this eloquent plea:

> Fellow-citizens, *we* cannot escape history. We of this

Congress and this administration, will be remembered in spite of ourselves. No personal significance, or insignificance, can spare one or another of us. The fiery trial through which we pass, will light us down, in honor or dishonor, to the latest generation. We *say* we are for the Union. The world will not forget that we say this. We know how to save the Union. The world knows we do know how to save it. We—even we here—hold the power, and bear the responsibility. In giving *freedom* to the *slave*, we *assure* freedom to the *free*—honorable alike in what we give, and what we preserve. We shall nobly save, or meanly lose, the last best hope of earth. Other means may succeed; this could not fail. The way is plain, peaceful, generous, just—a way which, if followed, the world will forever applaud, and God must forever bless.

This is a tremendous mobilization of pressure with words. And how universally true of each generation in its own way. Yet in the case in question the obstinate, war-distraught Congress (like the precarious Union-slave states) did not initiate the benign plan.

T. Harry Williams calls this "Message to Congress" of December 1, 1862, "the most finished literary document which Lincoln communicated to Congress. The plea for compensated emancipation and the description of the 'national homestead' [the Mississippi Valley] are among the best things he ever wrote."[33] Lincoln's concept that the Mississippi Valley *would* be a great nation and *would have* its outlet to the sea were not only his sincere Midwestern beliefs but his ultimate assertion of Southern hopelessness in undertaking secession.

Let us move back in time now to Lincoln's most memorable early work, the 1838 speech to the Springfield Young Men's Lyceum, "The Perpetuation of Our Political Institutions": Though containing a few youthful flights of patriotic rhetoric, it is still a very good speech to read today. It is a near-perfect rebuttal-in-advance to another angry young man's speech of a decade later, one widely read today as a source of a higher truth and morality than that of obedience to law, Thoreau's "Civil Disobedience." Lincoln, ever the champion of moderation, restraint, and gradualism, proclaims clearly the necessity of obeying the laws to preserve the whole fabric of faith in government, republican institutions, and the blessings of American freedom bequeathed us by a "departed race of ancestors." This view may seem trite today, but in the past decade of widespread organized civil disobedience for worldwide political and propaganda purposes (as well as legitimate reform) the effects Lincoln forecasts have been all too evident.

> Let reverence for the laws, be breathed by every American mother, to the lisping babe, that prattles on her lap—let it be taught in schools, in seminaries, and in colleges; let it be written in primers, spelling books, and in almanacs;—let it be preached from the pulpit, proclaimed in legislative halls, and enforced in courts of justice. And, in short, let it become the *political religion* of the nation; and let the old and the young, the rich and the poor, the grave and the gay, of all sexes and tongues, and colors and conditions, sacrifice unceasingly upon its altars.[34]

The man who loves the swing and sweep of words is not hard to find here. He goes on to leaven this absolute loyalty with encouragement for legislative reform where needed.

> ... let me not be understood as saying there are no bad laws ... bad laws, if they exist, should be repealed as soon as possible; still while they continue in force, for the sake of example, they should be religiously observed. So also in unprovided cases....[35]

This bit of rhetoric seems in its later portion to be (1) a rather unrealistic standard for the great American pragmatist and (2) a perfect expression of the irony of America, a government of laws created out of and revering a revolutionary heritage.

The most fascinating part of the speech is Lincoln's warning of the dangers of the likelihood of a future dictator, "some man possessed of the loftiest genius, coupled with ambition sufficient to push it to its utmost stretch."[36] Though Lincoln is doubtless thinking, as he claims, of a potential future Napoleon or Caesar—Hamilton's burning military ambition was well known to this devotee of Jefferson—yet the reader gets strong currents to support Edmund Wilson's conjecture that Lincoln was subconsciously projecting himself into this role.[37] In his later first few months as president, Lincoln certainly was a dictator; and the reader may recall Herndon's phrase about Lincoln's ambition: "a little engine that knew no rest."

> Towering genius disdains a beaten path. It seeks regions hitherto unexplored. . . . It thirsts and burns for distinction. . . . And when such a one does, it will require the people to be united with each other, attached to the government and laws, and generally intelligent, to successfully frustrate his designs.

Though the speech has one or two bad sentences, it has some grand literary passages. Basler reports that "James Weber Linn, in his 'Such Were His Words' (Abraham Lincoln Association Papers), claims that the third paragraph from the last was never surpassed by anything Lincoln ever wrote."[38] A few lines of the paragraph referred to[39] do ring with poetic power.

> But *those* histories [the living men of the Revolution] are gone. They can be read no more forever. They were a

fortress of strength; but, what invading foemen could never do, the silent artillery of time has done.

"The Perpetuation" was a worthy and timely piece of writing by a young unknown of twenty-nine in the state recently racked by the Elijah Lovejoy riots. And its thoughts on legal change, the fragility of republican governments before lawlessness or ambitious dictators, convey an important message to the militants and moderates of any age.

With the possible exception of his 1848 anti-Mexican War speech in Congress, Lincoln's next significant work was the Peoria speech of 1854 already mentioned. This is Lincoln's *tour de force* in attacking Douglas's Kansas-Nebraska law as an unwarranted and wrongheaded repeal of the Missouri Compromise. Though it is his longest speech (17,000 words), the last fifth of it is really a separate rebuttal-in-advance to Douglas's rebuttal, and should be omitted. The actual composed entity (the one he also gave at Springfield twelve days earlier) ends with the paragraph beginning "Our republican robe is soiled. . . . " In this work Lincoln clarifies the history of the event with incomparable brevity and motion—so well that it should be required reading for any student of United States history as well as students of public speaking. He gives example after example of blistering logic to explain to the audience, the state and the nation what is really happening with this disastrous legislation. He demonstrates how it is leading directly to the spread of slavery to all the territories, thence to all the states, and thus to the breakup, or total enslavement of the Union.

And if this fight [actual warfare in Kansas and Nebraska between abolitionist and pro-slavery forces] should begin, is it likely to take a very peaceful, Union-saving turn? Will not the first drop of blood so shed, be the real knell of the Union?[40]

144

He asserts also his basic concept that slavery should not be extended (because it is wrong, especially in a land of the free), but that where slavery exists it should be protected as part of the basic agreement of the United States Constitution (by implication until those states decide on their own that it is wrong and should be extinguished). He smashes Douglas's southern-supporting viewpoint over and over again, especially with the demonstration that each South Carolina white man equals two Maine white men in voting power. The Peoria speech, like the later "House Divided" and "Cooper Institute" addresses, reveals not only an eloquent speaker, clear thinker and good writer but a master scholar as well. The reader may examine Lincoln's short history of "what the Missouri Compromise is," paragraphs six through nineteen of the speech,[41] as vigorous example of Lincoln's effective stump scholarship.

And this Peoria speech reveals, too, the joyous warrior. He had found an issue he could fight all out for—and one that he, the clear thinker and master politician, could see could take him to the White House if he spurred the plunging electorate just right. In short, he could see Douglas taking one tack on the issue to get the presidency—so he, Lincoln, was challenged to take the other on the quite pragmatic assumption that there would be more votes for freeom than for slavery in the long run.

It is of interest to discover that Lincoln's greatest feat of writing and oratory is probably forever lost to us, except by description. Lincoln gave what was by all reports the greatest and most pivotal speech of his life at the Bloomington Convention, May 29, 1856. He did so as the last speaker of the day at a gathering to unify five rival factions (old Whigs, Free-Soilers, Know-Nothings, Anti-Nebraska Democrats, and abolitionists) into the second Republican Party.[42] This unification was successful, perhaps because of the magnetic effect of Lincoln's electrifying speech. That speech went unrecorded, reportedly because Lincoln's oratory was so astounding that even all the reporters and editors present stopped writing to listen. Skeptics suggest that Lincoln, planning violent oratory against slavery and secession, prevailed upon friendly members of the press to become so enthralled—so that strong quotations would not go abroad for later backlash.[43] It is at least true that Lincoln never provided anyone with a copy of what he said or planned to say. Though it is fascinating to speculate on what was said (and a dubious purported version of the speech was written out and published years later by Henry C. Whitney), no authentic manuscript is known. The effects of this episode are well summed up by Harry E. Pratt:

> This Bloomington speech in Major's Hall made Lincoln the Illinois leader of a new party, which within a year took possession of the State government, and four years later placed him at the head of the nation.[44]

Lincoln wrote well, too, in his "Dred Scott Decision" speech[45] delivered at Springfield, June 26, 1857. He gave a humorous total demolition of Douglas's support of Taney's interpretation of the Declaration of Independence as not applying to black people. The reader, while enjoying Lincoln's assaults, develops a sympathy for poor Douglas—being up against such a mental, political and oratorical smasher as Lincoln. The latter ends with:

> The plainest print cannot be read through a gold eagle; and it will be ever hard to find many men who will send a slave to Liberia, and pay his passage, while they can send him to a new country, Kansas, for instance, and sell him for fifteen hundred dollars and the rise.

The "House Divided" speech of June 16, 1858, is the classic presentation of Lincoln's prophetic assessment of the crisis

America was fast approaching. It is also his ultimate case against Douglas and the slave power for threatening the Union via a conspiracy to spread slavery to the territories and then all the states via another Dred Scott decision. It should be read in its entirety by anyone wishing to see Lincoln at his best. It threw down the gauntlet starting his campaign for Douglas's senate seat in Illinois, which led to the Lincoln-Douglas debates and national fame (though not the victory) for the tall Springfield lawyer. Listen to the rhythms of the opening:[46]

> If we could first know where we are, and whither we are tending, we could better judge what to do, and how to do it.
> We are now far into the fifth year, since a policy was initiated, with the avowed object, and confident promise, of putting an end to slavery agitation.
> Under the operation of that policy, that agitation has not only, not ceased, but has constantly augmented.
> In my opinion, it will not cease, until a crisis shall have been reached, and passed—
> "A house divided against itself cannot stand."
> I believe this government cannot endure, permanently half slave and half free.
> I do not expect the Union to be dissolved—I do not expect the house to fall—but I do expect it will cease to be divided.
> It will become all one thing, or all the other.

This is not just a candidate making a political speech. This is a poet working, a prophet writing new warnings from God for his own day.

After the "House Divided" and the debates, perhaps the best known prepresidential work of Lincoln is the address he made to the Young Men's Republican Union, February 27, 1860, at Cooper Institute in New York. This masterful speech convinced enough of the Eastern Republicans that Lincoln was a viable candidate, for him to win the forthcoming nomination. Here Lincoln surpasses the *Federalist Papers* in presenting a great lawyer's brief for his cause. It is a clear, organized, overwhelmingly thorough argument. Starting with Douglas's own words as text (that the founding fathers understood this slavery question better than we do now—and thus designed our half-slave half-free government to fit it), Lincoln destroys his opponent's position with a progressively building mountain of evidence ("actions speak louder than words") and beautiful refrains for repeated emphasis. Yet it is all in such clear, smooth-flowing language that no one in English can fail to understand.

The first half of the speech is also a masterpiece of tightly controlled scholarship. Lincoln does not delve into other related questions but sticks to his chosen task, destroying Douglas with his own words and proving the Democratic "Popular Sovereignty" doctrine to be basically unconstitutional and union-splitting. Yet the first part may be too legal and argumentative to be considered literature. Lincoln seemed to sense this, and after demolishing his opposition via an avalanche of scholarship, history and law, said, "But enough!" and launched into the second half, consisting of (1) a forthright appeal to the people of the South and (2) "A few words now to Republicans." In the former he needles the Southerners effectively for their errors in logic in becoming paranoid about the "Black Republican" party. He shows them in the clearest language the fallacies of their anti-Union, anti-moderate-Republican position. Slavery is protected in the slave states; all he wants to do is prevent its spread to the territories, something the federal government is clearly empowered to do as evidenced by the Northwest Ordinance of 1787 and several other limiting acts which he names. He punches a huge hole in the reasoning of the Dred Scott decision in the simplest and clearest language and therefore confidently expects its reversal.[47]

To show all this, is easy and certain.

When this obvious mistake of the Judges shall be brought to their notice, is it not reasonable to expect that they will withdraw the mistaken statement, and reconsider the conclusion based upon it?

The deft use of a question to gently present controversial interpretations is a device Lincoln used repeatedly. He had learned Franklin's trick of disguising his strongly held opinions in the form of suggestions.

Continuing to address the Southern people, he says:[48]

Under all these circumstances, do you really feel yourselves justified to break up this Government unless such a court decision as yours is, shall be at once submitted to as a conclusive and final rule of political action? But you will not abide the election of a Republican president! In that supposed event, you say, you will destroy the Union; and then, you say, the great crime of having destroyed it will be upon us! That is cool. A highwayman holds a pistol to my ear, and mutters through his teeth, "Stand and deliver, or I shall kill you, and then you will be a murderer!"

His powerful finale reveals the only Republican actions which can never be acceptable to the South: *saying and thinking* that slavery is in any way wrong.[49]

Holding, as they do, that slavery is morally right, and socially elevating, they cannot cease to demand a full national recognition of it, as a legal right, and a social blessing.

On the grounds of morality, then, he rallies Republicans and all those opposed to the expansion of slavery not to give in to the highwayman but to stand firm. Echoing Patrick Henry, he closes with an all-caps shout: "LET US HAVE FAITH THAT RIGHT MAKES MIGHT, AND IN THAT FAITH, LET US, TO THE END, DARE TO DO OUR DUTY AS WE UNDERSTAND IT." A fierce, warlike battle cry, gently disguised as the highest morality.

The "First Inaugural Address," March 4, 1861, is considered one of Lincoln's finest pieces. It is the kindly appeal to the South for union and peace with a guarantee of no interference with slavery in the slave states and of enforcement of the fugitive slave law throughout the nation. It is quiet passion on the desperate need for union (for continuing the bizarre marriage of North and South). But it is also firm against the extension of slavery into the new territories and for United States determination to fight if the South insists on secession (already an accomplished fact by the time of the inauguration). It echoes in the most diplomatic terms the one sentence recorded from the "Lost Speech" of 1856: "We will say to the Southern disunionists, 'We won't go out of the Union, and you shan't!' "[50] It is a firm, clear peace offering, arguing eloquently, guaranteeing rights but not surrendering or threatening. Lincoln demonstrates how secession, once accepted, will breed further secession; and he states again the base idea of his 1838 Lyceum speech while echoing Locke, Adams, and Jefferson:[51]

Plainly, the central idea of secession, is the essence of anarchy. A majority, held in restraint by constitutional checks and limitations, and always changing easily with deliberate changes of popular opinions and sentiments is the only true sovereign of a free people. Whoever rejects it, does, of necessity, fly to anarchy or to despotism. Unanimity is impossible; the rule of a minority, as a permanent arrangement, is wholly inadmissible; so that, rejecting the majority principle, anarchy or despotism in some form is all that is left.

He defends the legal basis for the Union, showing how the concept predated the Declaration of Independence and the Constitutional Convention of 1787, each of these steps leading to the improvement of a perpetual entity, "a more perfect union." He lays out the terrible course of war—and shows how ultimately both sides will just have to heal up what they now may needlessly inflict upon each other. And he presents a last ringing appeal[52] for loyalty to the tradition of union which is so deep within all our people.

In *your* hands, my dissatisfied fellow countrymen, and not in *mine*, is the momentous issue of civil war. The government will not assail *you*. You can have no conflict, without being yourselves the aggressors. *You* have no oath registered in Heaven to destroy the government, while *I* shall have the most solemn one to "preserve, protect and defend" it.

I am loth to close. We are not enemies, but friends. We must not be enemies. Though passion may have strained, it must not break our bonds of affection. The mystic chords of memory, stretching from every battle-field, and patriot grave, to every living heart and hearth-stone, all over this broad land, will yet swell the chorus of the Union, when again touched, as surely they will be, by the better angels of our nature.

Basler demonstrates Lincoln's artistry in reworking Seward's suggestions for this ending, aimed at making it less militant than the first draft. The side-by-side presentation of Seward's suggestions and Lincoln's reworking shows clearly the prose-poet in action.[53]

Any explanation of Lincoln's Gettysburg Address mocks itself by being longer and less gracefully written than the model being studied. It also runs the risk in many minds of tampering with a sacred institution (as an architect might by pacing off a cathedral while religious services were being held) and thus being downright blasphemous. Furthermore, it pits the critic against all previous exponents of rhetoric and literary art who have dissected these three moving paragraphs to get at the secret of their power. Setting these risks as far back in his mind as possible, this writer presents his answers to the question, What is so all-fired great about the Gettysburg Address?

(The reader is urged here to reread the page in question. See Appendix B.)

Compression: These ten sentences are primarily effective for the many things Lincoln does in so short a space:

1. He clarifies in one sentence the essential meaning of the United States: "a new nation . . . dedicated to the proposition [as in debate] that all men are created equal"—not equal in ability but in dignity before the law and hence in opportunity for justice, gain, education, advancement, for making their own most desired choices insofar as these do not infringe upon the rights of others. Lincoln also implies the basic method of this nation for reaching its high goal: government of the people, by the people, for the people, i.e., representative democracy. But as the opening sentence sketches a nation dedicated to a debatable proposition, so it also poses to the reader or listener the possibility that the proposition must be proved by performance—by the success of the experiment.

2. In sentence two he clarifies the essential meaning of the Civil War, the most severe trial to date of the grand experiment, "testing whether that nation . . . can long endure." This rending war (hundreds of thousands dead already, on both sides—Americans all) will obviously kill or prove the strength of the new continent-sized super-nation dedicated to republican principles; will lead on to the undreamed of "vast future of man" or the petty Balkanization of North America.

3. By sentence three and four he ties the two related abstractions above to the immediate occasion: the dedication

152

of a national cemetery honoring the 51,000 men who fell in what was recognized as one of the decisive battles of this war. "We are met on a great battlefield of that war. We have come to dedicate a portion of that field, as a final resting place for those who here gave their lives that that nation might live." Note that he does not honor only the Union dead, but leaves it open that all who fell in the battle (Americans north and south) might be included in the honors due the brave men willing to die for their concept of country. Thus he leaves the door open as always for the healing of the Union. Since the size and significance of this battle is well known to his audience (especially after a two-hour main address by Edward Everett)—since the graves were all about and signs of battle still defaced the ground[54]—Lincoln needed no elaboration here.

4. He shows fit respect for the dead being commemorated (their sacrifice) by suitable self-deprecation of *us*, the living, versus *them*, the dead—and least of all, these flimsy words. "The world will little note nor long remember what we say here, but it can never forget what they did here." The words proved to be ironic of course, since, in fact, the reverse is closer to the facts of history—due solely to Lincoln's power as a writer. Yet with what Barzun has indicated of Lincoln's conscious literary genius,[55] it is hard to believe that Lincoln did not intentionally make that effect of his words take place.

5. He uses the combination of the two foregoing abstractions and two specifics (the battle and today's dedication) to rally his listeners and readers, "us the living," to take from these great ideas, events and sacrifices, inspiration (increased devotion, high resolve) to do in honor of them what we *can* do: finish the unfinished work (of both the war and the great experiment).

6. The possibility of finishing the great experiment successfully leads the reader to a higher abstraction than points 1 or 2: the idea that success in America's experiment in self-government will prove that system's efficacy as a potential for

all men. Thus, America's success in this battle, this war, this grand century of experiment, is more important than just the life of one nation, the present people of North and South. It is the trial of an idealistic dream (self-government of the people) that, if practical in the American case, gives "promise [from his Independence Hall speech] that in due time the weights should be lifted from all men, and that *all* should have an equal chance." This theme is not without indicators in the first five lines: "conceived in liberty"; "dedicated ... that all men are created equal"; "testing whether ... any nation so conceived and so dedicated can long endure." Yet in these early lines the highest abstraction is so blended with the lesser ones as to not yet dominate. Only with the final lines, "that government of the people, by the people, for the people, shall not perish from the earth," does it emerge as the central idea. This central idea, of course, is a spiritualization of politics, government, law and even war, based on Lincoln's belief (like Jefferson's) that republicanism should be "the political religion of the nation." It is the basis of Jeremy Bentham's "greatest good for the greatest number" (to which Lincoln added, "in the long run") extended to a worldwide basis, and is heavy with the ideas of an American-led chosen people and one world of freedom. Yet it continues to hold its magnetism for men and women everywhere, not just Americans,[56] because it is essentially true. The United States has always been and continues to be an unparalleled and innovative example of the power of people freed from unnecessary institutional restraints on their thoughts, words and deeds. Despite all its flaws, weaknesses and wartime disasters, America stands, as Lincoln rightly saw, for the individual against any institutionalized tyranny, and as such, by example, strengthens the concept of dynamic world order based on freedom and responsibility—and thus the ultimate good of all survivors of the various struggles.

7. In addition to packing the foregoing six ideas into his ten sentences, Lincoln has also planted within and throughout his

154

entity a subtle Christian metaphor which unifies the whole and increases the dimension of it as an expression of national spiritual salvation. With the King James Bible rhythms throughout (Four score and seven years), the prophetic tone, the *conceived* and *brought forth* and *dedicated* so like human conception, birth and religious baptism, with the benediction-like affirmation at the close, this intentional Father Abraham (who knew his task of leadership was "greater than that which rested on Washington") is clearly ("under God") leading his nation in prayer. (The crisis was still very much before them in November, 1863.) But he is also adroitly transferring to the nation the same concept of spiritual rebirth that Christians believe is necessary for personal salvation. (As Nicodemus asked, "What do you mean, reborn?") As the "new nation" had been a babe when brought forth by "our fathers" on this continent, "conceived in liberty," and had grown and matured for "four score and seven years," so it now had finally reached a spiritual crisis based on whether it could accept or not its own ideals that "all men are created equal" and that "government of the people, by the people, for the people" was a workable system. Since the now mature nation had discovered its own evils of slavery and secession (in effect minority rule)—its own sins—it was now suffering a climax of trial, repentence, suffering and death. Yet this suffering, like that of Job, was part of our necessary grief for spiritual redemption—provided we could go through it and stay loyal "under God" to "the better angels of our natures"—i.e., our devotion to the democratic ideals of our founding fathers. Thus from this "great civil war" would come, if we were true, the Christian idea of spiritual rebirth, and we as a nation would have (Lincoln shows his confidence and determination by using *shall have*) "a new birth of freedom" (no more slavery, republicanism justified as a viable form of government, now cleaner, freer than before)—and this higher kind of nation will go on to fulfill its destiny of leading by successful example all men to freedom. This subtle tour de force of metaphor,

155

admittedly more fully developed in the "Second Inaugural," is achieved through just a handful of words. Yet it is clearly planted here by the two binding, framing, theme-forming phrases, "conceived in liberty" (repeated *so conceived*) and "a new birth of freedom." It is the apotheosis of American democracy as a step in God's harsh cultivation of his chosen people, his harsh pruning of his own vine, for the benefit of all mankind.

The assertion of all the foregoing accomplishment in twenty-four lines may seem a gratuitous glorification of Lincoln as artist (when the artistic devices have not even been mentioned yet). But perhaps an indirect proof that Lincoln knew what he was about could be adduced from quoting again Lincoln's 1859 praise of Jefferson on the Declaration of Independence[57] with substitutions made via line-throughs and brackets of phrases which could apply the same remarks to Lincoln as conscious artist at Gettysburg:

> All honor to ~~Jefferson~~ [Lincoln]—to the man who in the concrete pressure of a struggle for national ~~independence~~ [survival] by a single people, had the coolness, forecast, and capacity to introduce into a merely ~~revolutionary~~ [dedicatory] document, an abstract truth, and so to embalm it there, that today, and in all coming days, it shall be a rebuke and a stumbling block to the very harbingers of reappearing tyranny and oppression.

There is no question that there is the ring of the prophet as well as the poet and critic in those lines. And there is no question that what Lincoln could recognize of literary greatness in Jefferson in 1859 he would be striving to emulate or surpass in 1863.

Simplicity: The Gettysburg Address also is effective for its unpretentious simplicity. As with all Lincoln writing, it is completely understandable to any sympathetic reader, intellectual and average man alike. The abstractions, though profound, come through to the reader with utmost clarity. Though he does not shun large or formal words (*proposition, dedicated, consecrate*), he uses them in such a way that no obfuscation is possible; and his emphasis, as Basler points out,[58] is on the simplest words: *we* (the living); *they* (these honored dead); *here* (this great battlefield); and what *we* should therefore highly *resolve.*

Understatement: With rigid control of his material, Lincoln uses understatement to the maximum. He gives not one glorifying sentence to the valiant deeds of the soldiers. You see not one wounded soldier, not one charging battle flag, not one weeping mother or infant, not one hero killed bringing the cup of water to his dying comrade. Least of all you see no praise for individual generals or units, no credit taken by the administration or Lincoln himself, no praise given particular states or even the North as a nation. No politicking is done, and the voice is like that of a detached prophet expressing the grief yet the hope-through-the-grief of the nation.

Grace: Lincoln, in spite of his passion for brevity, has a simultaneous passion for the eloquent beat of rhythm, rhyme, alliteration, repetition, resonance, echoings, and balanced phrases and sentences in emphasizing his terse thoughts.

conceived in liberty	so *conceived* and so dedicated
new *nation*	that *nation,* or any nation

dedicated to the proposition
  so conceived and so *dedicated*
    we have come to *dedicate*
    we cannot *dedicate*

It is for us the living . . . *to be dedicated*
. . . to be here *dedicated* to the great task

} In a brief speech of dedication.

... we cannot dedicate—we cannot consecrate—we cannot hallow this ground [yet with these rhythmic incantations am I hallowing it]. The brave men, living and dead, have consecrated it....

Lincoln's use of commas and dashes, to force the reader to pause when and where he wants him to pause—so that he will listen to the sound the words make on his spirit—is part of his rich application of the poet's art. In short, this cannot be considered a speech, or a talk, or a few remarks. It is unquestionably a poem—any word or phrase removed or rearranged causing a weakening of the poem's powerful effect. His sense of ear and fitness even caused him to drop an extraneous word and add "under God" while speaking, as the last polishing took place in the heat of the occasion.[59] Lincoln has in fact written here a new psalm of America—one intuitively recognized as great through its sweeping vision, clarity of meaning, and the magnetic rhythms of the poet's art.

Significance and Universality: The significance of the poem and its universality have already been discussed under *Compression,* yet each shows not only Lincoln's remarkable insight but his swift ability to make that insight clear and acceptable to the reader. And his successful raising of the nationalistic struggle to the level of the worldwide, age-old human struggle for selfhood and fulfillment affirms his capacity as seer as well as merely national leader or poet. It is this vision, plus his ability to translate this vision into practical advances through action, for which Lincoln is revered around the world as a major builder of the grand "family of man."

An examination of the first, second and final drafts of this two-minute incantation (presented in Roy P. Basler, ed., *Abraham Lincoln: His Speeches and Writings,* 734-7) gives the reader a healthy regard for how even what comes to be revered as national literature is written by a single breathing man, with a pen, scratching out words to improve his expression just as do ordinary men. For example, the change from (first draft) "that the nation might live," to (second draft) "that that nation might live," clearly improves the emphasis. Again (first draft): "This we may, in all propriety do," is definitely improved in grace though lengthened in words by becoming, "It is altogether fitting and proper that we should do this." Again, in the change from (second draft) "and that this government of the people." to (final draft) "and that government of the people," the dropping of one word, *this,* enlarges the meaning from the simply national application to the worldwide, from that of the present to that of all future time.

The ultimate reason the Gettysburg Address is considered great rhetorical art is that it is intuitively accepted as a true rendering of a multiplex idea, embodied in the most graceful language—language that every reader and listener in English can readily understand. Its widespread acceptance in Western civilization also stems from the religious nature of man (an engine behind much of poetry's power), his appreciative embrace of inspiring expression of his best social ideal, "that *all* should have an equal chance."

The "Second Inaugural Address," March 4, 1865, enlarges the noble themes launched and reiterated in the "Independence Hall Speech" and the Gettysburg Address. "Let us strive to finish the work we are in"—the war, the experiment, the grand release of prisoners that is America. With the same kind of restraint, understatement, brevity and poetic art—yet, indeed, with an elation of spirit—Lincoln explains "this terrible war" and perhaps throws a comforting light on all war and suffering that afflict mankind.

Pursuing the ideas in his previous fragments, "Meditation on the Divine Will" (1862) and "On Slavery" (1858), Lincoln suggests that the war's suffering on both sides may be God's just vengeance on the white men of both North and South for "the bond-man's two hundred and fifty years of unrequited toil." Yet if this is so, we cannot but still find that God is, in the psalmist David's words, "true and righteous altogether." Here was an extension of the Old and New Testaments being spoken from the Capitol in Washington, 1865.

In melodic sentences we read a theological explanation of the meaning and necessity of war by the poet-president who had suffered war almost as fully as had any other survivor.[60]

> The Almighty has his own purposes. "Woe unto the world because of offenses! for it must needs be that offenses come; but woe to that man by whom the offense cometh!" If we shall suppose that American slavery is one of those offenses which, in the providence of God, must needs come, but which, having continued through His appointed time, He now wills to remove, and that He gives to both North and South, this terrible war, as the woe due to those by whom the offense came, shall we discern therein any departure from those divine attributes which the believers in a Living God always ascribe to him?

Certainly there is nothing false about Lincoln's use of biblical rhythms, quotations, and allusions, nothing insincere or dogmatic in his explanation of why we may have been given this indescribable suffering. Yet he does not stop there. He turns the inaugural address, usually a ceremonial rite used for inspirational rallying, into a national prayer. "Fondly do we hope—fervently do we pray—that this mighty scourge of war may speedily pass away." And the explanation continues—but gently, in the form of a possibility, not a dogmatic assertion. If God wills us to pay such an awful price as this war for our age-old evils, can we yet call him unjust? Then comes the rallying, not to join in triumph over the prostrate South, but to enlist help from all in healing these afflictions, generating the

160

positive forgiveness necessary from all to renew this nation as a cleansed land worthy of her heritage.

He ends with a radiant constructive confidence that we as a nation have emerged from these searing fires and will be able, with forgiveness and resurgent love, "to bind up the nation's wounds—to care for him who shall have borne the battle . . . and achieve a just and lasting peace, among ourselves, and with all nations." As such this two-page masterpiece is a paean of hope to a wounded people, another great poem disguised as a state paper, yet also a suggestion of religious revelation of universal significance.

All the abilities of the poet are unleashed in this orchestrated production. From the genial, modest beginning, to the explanatory paragraph two (teaching in apparently neutral fashion how the South actually did start the war, of course), to a more serious explanation of slavery's role, the word-artist is building to his passionate conclusion of paragraph three.

Both read the same Bible, and pray to the same God; and each invokes His aid against the other. It may seem strange that any men should dare to ask a just God's assistance in wringing their bread from the sweat of other men's faces; but let us judge not that we be not judged.

From there to paragraph's end it is a symphony of anger, justice, righteousness and suffering due to individual and collective sins over generations of time—discovered finally to be cleansed and forgiven at last by the stern fires of a loving God. Then the last paragraph is the fine gold of Job's reaffirmation of faith, the kindness emanating from the saved spirit—which this nation must now have, having survived its trial. His magnificent poem is ended. Another piece of American scripture has been written.

Lincoln wrote other works almost as good, fitting his basic pattern of ideas to other occasions—the letter to Mrs. Bixby, the letter to James C. Conkling (really a short speech to be delivered in Springfield by that gentleman in lieu of Lincoln), the "Last Public Address," urging forgiveness to get the Confederate state of Louisiana back into the working Union. But perhaps Lincoln's finest, most succinct work is the page and a half of extemporaneous remarks he uttered at Independence Hall,[61] on Washington's Birthday, 1861, as he journeyed to the nation's capital:

I have often inquired of myself what great principle or idea it was that kept this confederacy so long together. It was not the mere matter of the separation of the colonies from the motherland; but that sentiment in the Declaration of Independence which gave . . . promise that in due time the weights should be lifted from the shoulders of all men, and that *all* should have an equal chance. . . .

Now, my friends, can this country be saved upon that basis? If it can, I will consider myself one of the happiest men in the world if I can help to save it. If it can't be saved upon that principle . . . —I was about to say I would rather be assassinated on this spot than to surrender it. . . .

My friends, this is a wholly unprepared speech. I did not expect to be called upon to say a word when I came here—I supposed I was merely to do something towards raising a flag. I may, therefore, have said something indiscreet, but I have said nothing but what I am willing to live by, and, in the pleasure of Almighty God, die by.

Lincoln's literary achievement, then, was essentially the carrying on, the rejuvenation, of the literary-political achievement of Jefferson, which is no less than the articulation of the grand function of the United States in the world. This process

162

is perhaps best expressed in Lincoln's "Fragment on the Constitution and Union" [1860?][62]

> The expression of that principle ["liberty to all"] in our Declaration of Independence, was most happy, and fortunate. Without this, as well as with it, we could have declared our independence of Great Britain; but without it, we could not, I think, have secured our free government, and consequent prosperity. No oppressed people will fight, and endure, as our fathers did, without the promise of something better, than a mere change of masters.

Hence Lincoln's literary achievement was no less than that of providing the words and the moral leadership for a national and worldwide expansion of the American Revolution.

Theodore Roosevelt (signature)

Theodore Roosevelt
Writer at Full Gallop

He entered into men's lives, kindled fires in them, im-
pelled them to scorn ease and safety and rejoice to do
the fine, the difficult thing.[1]

Hermann Hagedorn

Theodore Roosevelt (1858-1919), twenty-fifth president of
the United States (1901-1909), is known for almost everything
except his considerable body of writing. He is known for such
roles as those of brash nationalist; seizer of Panama; buck-
tooth buffoon; "big stick" warmonger (who paradoxically
kept us out of war as president and won the Nobel Peace Prize
for helping end the Russo-Japanese War); trust-buster of the
Progressive era; Bull Moose maverick Republican who,
despite himself, helped elect Woodrow Wilson by starting a
third party; big game hunter and naturalist; conservationist
who greatly enlarged the National Forests and the public

consciousness of the importance of saving parks, wildlife and range; rousing, fast-walking physical culturist who reflected near-fascist admiration for the "manly virtues." Yet few except historians know of his constant writing, speaking, publishing, editorializing, and serious historical and naturalist study, his interesting magazine articles and moral essays, that came in a continual stream for forty years amidst all his other activity. He was a Harvard graduate (Phi Beta Kappa); a law student; a member of the New York State Legislature (where in three years he became a leader of the reform wing of the Republicans); a cattle rancher in the Dakota Territory for three years; an unsuccessful candidate for mayor of New York in 1886; a member of the Civil Service Commission for six years; a New York City police commissioner for two years; an assistant secretary of the Navy for one year; a lieutenant colonel, First U. S. Volunteer Cavalry Regiment (Rough Riders) for the four-month Cuban campaign; governor of New York, two years (with much reform work accomplished); vice-president under McKinley; and, upon the assassination of McKinley, September, 1901, president of the United States.

A glance at a list of Theodore Roosevelt's main works (Appendix C) will show that he was the most prolific writer among American statesmen. He wrote thirty-three volumes on numerous subjects (eight genres as listed here) plus 150,000 letters, numerous pamphlets, articles, essays and speeches. He was not only America's most rambunctious president but one of the most widely read men of his time—in both senses of that term. Besides being a vigorous reformer and political leader (eight major offices), he was a noteworthy orator, naturalist, historian, conservationist, hunter, military leader, diplomat and moralist. He earned his titles of "trust-buster," builder of the Panama Canal, "driver of the band-wagon," leader of a "new nationalism," Nobel Peace Prize winner, father of conservation, soft-walker with a big stick, and champion of "the strenuous life." (See any of the biographies of TR listed in the Bibliography.) The reader interested in TR's books may choose from autobiography, essay, hunting and travel, biography, history, natural history, selected letters, national politics and international relations, or selections from all the foregoing types. This writer intends to present a sketch of TR as writer as well as a glimpse of each type of his work with a few recommendations for the reader's consideration. As to defending the innate quality of the samples recommended, or setting up any comparative quality chart, it might be well to recall TR's own words when asked to do the same for his famous sixty-volume "pigskin library" taken on one hunting trip:

> I like very many and very different kinds of books, and do not for a moment attempt anything so preposterous as a continual comparison between books that may appeal to totally different sets of emotions. . . . I do not quarrel with the taste of the critic in question, but I see no reason why anyone should be guided by it.[2]

Though Theodore Roosevelt was a thoroughly competent and interesting writer in his own right (he had published seven creditable volumes before becoming known politically outside his own state), one has to admit that his fame as a writer then as now was enhanced by his meteoric political success from the beginning. (This of course is true while it is also true that the successful hunter-historian-writer was aiding the brilliant young New York legislator to become better known, more popular and respected.) Furthermore, as editor William Harbaugh points out in the *Writings of Theodore Roosevelt*, "it was his political career that gives his writings historical [and one might add, biographical] significance."[3] His books, though almost all readable in their own right, are of more interest to the present-day reader for the light they shed on this remarkable man's versatility, energy and mind (and the values revered in his time) than they are for their own sake. Though in *The Winning of the West* and *Ranch Life and the*

Hunting Trail he presented historical and personal narratives of fine accuracy, imagery and readability, we would be unlikely to go back to them now if the author's name were not Theodore Roosevelt.

It is only fair to add that one of the genuine values of reading TR is to discover the genuine thinker within the doer, the man of mind within the man of action, the man who not only sustained for forty years a nearly incredible record of performance of deeds but who simultaneously was a man who read everything, current, classical and historical, and who also was one of the major producing writers of his day. In short, TR's main interest to the modern reader may be that of an energy phenomenon, an example of the capability of the completely integrated personality (even one with an originally sickly body), a nearly contemporary Renaissance man in the day of electric turbines, industrial trusts and battleship war, a modern example of the philosopher-king—though poles apart from Plato in philosophy.

Theodore Roosevelt has been so fixed in the public mind by cartoons and thumbnail treatments and the quotation of his warmongering statements of the 1890s and 1900s that not much is known of his actually wide-ranging thought. As Harbaugh sums up,

> It is his enduring misfortune that his more grievous verbal and operational excesses are better remembered than his substantial service to world peace and his monumental contributions to progressivism.[4]

Though in some ways his philosophy was simple-minded (decisions social, political and international were merely matters of choosing good over evil, manliness over effeminacy, the public good over the private gain, hard duty over pleasurable corruption); yet he was correct in assessing man's basic problems as moral rather than intellectual or merely technical. (The real difficulty was not in how to get to the moon; it was in how to best spend our economic and technical resources in a multilevel world of intricate, interrelated problems for the best social, economic and spiritual return.) Though TR was of the seventh generation of a line of Dutch-American Manhattan merchants, though he was of the wealthy, Republican, Harvard-educated elite, though he was a city-and-culture man through and through, he, like all great politicians, had a most perceptive sense of the pulse and needs of the common people in his time and place. If there was an elitism at all in TR, it was one based on morality, honor, manliness, the advancement of culture (degree of "civilization"), nationalism, and progressivism, not on education or intellectual or artistic merit per se. It was not Jefferson's natural aristocracy of talent and virtue but a TR *noblesse oblige* based on personal character; love of the common man; courage; exercise; preparedness (willingness to fight at need); loyalty to the nation, the race and western civilization; support of fidelity in marriage; motherhood (literally); and the will to improve society through initiative, cooperation, new organizational experiments and doing one's duty.

There was, of course, much of Don Quixote in this romantic, resounding, moralizing, hard-charging, chest-beating and at times infantile nationalist. This may be shown by his discovery in the jungles of Cuba near San Juan Hill that a cavalry officer charging through the brush on foot in modern war is likely to get his feet entangled in his sword.[5] Yet the point of the episode is that he learned from the fiasco and thereafter left the sword in the baggage. And he went on to blunder to admirable success in the fight, and was prevented by an irate War Department from getting a deserved high decoration for his services apparently because he joined other disgruntled officers in signing a successful protest to get the troops moved out of the fever area before disease destroyed them.[6] Not only the American pragmatist, but the realist (Sancho Panza), emerged often, too, as when he championed the rights of working girls not to get their arms cut off by

169

unsafe factory machines because the courts had overprotected property rights. Justice not legalism from the law was his lifelong fight.[7]

The character of the man can be drawn quickly from a sampling of his writing, though it is only fair to him to take samples from his more experienced presidential and post-presidential writing to see how his character matured from his earlier Nietzsche-like Anglo-Saxon race-nationalism into a highly responsible, innovative-yet-moderate Americanism. He had a lifelong war with critics who could carp but not *do* half as well as the target of their criticism, a passion for practicing what he preached. Words not backed up by action, precept without performance, threats or bluff made without the ability and will to make them good were worse than useless. They were not merely hypocrisy (a moral crime), but they were destructive in the everyday world, causing misconceptions, errors, miscalculation, wars, the encouragement of crime and corruption, destruction of every sort. When Roosevelt detected that the war party in Japan believed him to be now afraid of Japanese defeat of the American fleet, he sent the latter around the world (right by Japan) to correct their misconception.[8] Peace with Japan was thus assured for another third of a century.

He also had a passion for plain speaking, the ringing phrase, imagery in writing, the coining of slogans, soundness of research, the production of (and the reading of) *interesting* writing, a thirst for the spectacular and the valiant test, for a rousing family life, and a catholic taste in books. He felt the greatest cowardice to be the fear of living (that is, living richly, bravely, boldly) and the fear of dying or suffering in the struggle. Yet he swallowed his burning military ambition (his Viking yearning for the chance to die a hero in battle) when Wilson would not appoint him an officer of a volunteer division in World War I (250,000 men expressed a willingness to serve under him!)[9] and dutifully took up his pen to be the most constructive critic of Wilson's policies in sometimes

170

blistering editorials for the *Kansas City Star*.[10]

Theodore Roosevelt's style is usually swift, blunt, direct, vigorous—and thus appealing to the common man despite its often being considered simplistic or jingoistic by intellectuals or political opponents. Yet through his ability to think and write clearly, TR delivers quite perceptive and subtle thoughts in language everyone can understand:

I have always maintained that our worst revolutionaries today are those reactionaries who do not see and will not admit that there is any need for change.[11]

Occasionally he is bombastic or overstated: "The day when the keels of the low-Dutch sea-thieves first grated on the British coast was big with the doom of many nations."[12] He launches into the language many sloganesque phrases that, though they soon become clichés, often are apt and vivid expressions: "Bull Moose"; "big stick"; "square deal"; "new nationalism"; "social and industrial justice"; "criminals of the wealthy classes." He detests "weasel-words" or vague political smokescreen phraseology. In criticizing Point Eight of Wilson's Fourteen Points ("All French territory should be freed and the invaded portions restored, and the wrong done to France by Prussia in 1871 in the matter of Alsace-Lorraine which has unsettled the peace of the world for nearly fifty years, should be righted, in order that peace may once more be made secure in the interest of all.") TR writes:

Point eight deals with Alsace-Lorraine and is couched in language which betrays Mr. Wilson's besetting sin— his inability to speak in a straightforward manner. He may mean that Alsace and Lorraine must be restored to France, in which case his is right. He may mean that a plebiscite must be held, in which case he is playing Germany's evil game.[13]

It is possible to detect TR's strong affinity for Lincoln's writing as well as Lincoln's point of view and clarity in thinking in the foregoing passage. TR is often irritating to today's reader because of his dogmatic statement, self-righteousness, and white race consciousness, while nevertheless writing with ringing power and no little accuracy:

> The warlike borderers who thronged across the Alleghenies, the restless and reckless hunters, the hard, dogged, frontier farmers, by dint of grim tenacity overcame and displaced Indians, French, and Spaniards alike, exactly as, fourteen hundred years before, Saxon and Angle had overcome and displaced the Cymric and Gaelic Celts. They were led by no one commander; they acted under orders from neither king nor congress; they were not carrying out the plans of any far-sighted leader. In obedience to the instincts working half-blindly within their breasts, spurred ever onward by the fierce desires of their eager hearts, they made in the wilderness homes for their children, and by so doing wrought out the destinies of a continental nation.[14]

His style, in short, aims at readability, image-filled smooth-flowing narration, Lincolnesque simplicity, with little attempt to check (indeed, on the contrary, with strong intention to use) his enthusiasms of spirit in the interests of literary effect.

It is useful to look briefly at some of the TR bibliography as listed in Appendix C: The *Autobiography* (1913) is perhaps the best single piece of TR to read if one has time and interest for reading only one of his books. Written at the right time in life and before any failure of skill or slowing of pace became evident,[15] the *Autobiography* contains swift readable glimpses of all facets of his multifarious career—all save the story of his love for and his life with his first wife, Alice Lee. Because of her tragic death in giving birth to Alice Roosevelt in 1884, followed within twelve hours by the death of TR's own mother, he chose to drop out of New York life for three years to do western cattle ranching and omit these sad personal episodes from his own life story. When the *Autobiography* was republished in a 1958 centennial edition, editor Wayne Andrews cut it slightly and supplemented it here and there with passages of TR's other writings (including a tender memorial to his first wife). These additions help fill in such blanks as well as give glimpses through letters of the warlike and antiliberal TR to counter the vigorous virtue of his own side of the story.

The chapter headings alone provide a swift synopsis of the life and its many interesting facets: "Boyhood and Youth"; "The Vigor of Life"; "Practical Politics"; "In Cowboy Land"; "Applied Idealism"; "The New York Police"; "The War of America the Unready"; "The New York Governorship"; "Outdoors and Indoors"; "The Presidency: Making an Old Party Progressive"; "The Natural Resources of the Nation"; "The Big Stick and the Square Deal"; "Social and Industrial Justice"; "The Monroe Doctrine and the Panama Canal"; "The Peace of Righteousness"; "Hunter and Historian"; "Armageddon and Afterward."

He writes and thinks vigorously, explains himself clearly, always establishes his individual personality and keeps surprising and pleasing the reader with his initiative, merit, and real devotion to duty, virtue, "realizable ideals." His frequent moral homilies, though perhaps irritating, are usually unarguable. The negative aspects of his character are his authoritarianism, his self-righteousness, jingoism, belligerence, his love of war as strengthening and virtuous, a childish, if not Nazi, attitude revealing one large motive of war—as a desirable theatre for action to express male sexual prowess or hormonal courage (female-impressing manliness) and never mind all those people who get killed; (they are the weaklings, cowards and traitors anyway, aren't they—and better off wiped out). The just irony of his life was that he lived to see his beloved little boy, Quentin, die as a man in the air war over France (though not his older son, Ted, who died in France in the later war in 1944); yet TR was frustrated in his own ambition to lead a division, and perhaps die in battle, due to Woodrow Wilson's stubborn refusal to appoint him, supposedly on grounds of age and the needs of the military for greater professional knowledge. Nevertheless, in response to Quentin's death, TR wrote one of his finest essays, "The Great Adventure," for *Metropolitan Magazine:*

> Unless men are willing to fight and die for great ideals, including love of country, ideals will vanish, and the world will become one huge sty of materialism.[16]

TR was perhaps at his best and most significant as he sought a middle road between laissez faire America and socialism through his program of progressive reform to control the rampant monster-corporations and promote labor unions in the public interest.

> Men who understand and practice the deep underlying philosophy of the Lincoln school of American political thought are necessarily Hamiltonian in their belief in a strong and efficient National Government and Jeffersonian in their belief in the people as the ultimate authority, and in the welfare of the people as the end of government.[17]

> ... It did not seem to me that the law was framed to discourage as it should sharp practice...[18]

On the abuse of the concept of constitutionalism in the robber baron era TR wrote:

> These businessmen and lawyers...made it evident that they valued the Constitution, not as a help to righteousness, but as a means for thwarting movements against unrighteousness.[19]

A democracy can be such in fact only if there is some rough approximation to similarity in stature among the men composing it.... But a rich and complex industrial society cannot so exist; for some individuals, and especially those artificial individuals called corporations, become so very big that the ordinary individual is utterly dwarfed beside them, and cannot deal with them on terms of equality. It therefore becomes necessary for these ordinary individuals to combine in their turn, first in order to act in their collective capacity through that biggest of all combinations called the government, and second, to act, also in their own self-defense, through private combinations, such as farmers' associations and trade unions.[20]

Ranch Life and the Hunting Trail, published in 1888 (before fame had found the progressive leader), is a fine, readable book, a series of autobiographical, yet subject-focused chapters on TR's experiences on the remote cattle ranges of the Little Missouri River of the Dakota Territory in the years 1884 through 1886. Upon TR's insistence, the work was illustrated by the great Frederick Remington; and together they give a marvelous series of glimpses of that last phase of the old frontier, between the conquest of the horse tribes of the plains and the fenced ranches of a later day. It is a worthwhile contribution to local color literature. TR reveals here his essence as a writer—a participant in interesting living and his perceptive observations thereof. These two traits make for worthy chronicles of the plains and mountain life, intimate glimpses of cowboys, miners, Indians, hunters, the plains women, game animals and the changing west just after the cattlemen had moved in. He constantly presents items revealing the inner psyche of the men being described; for example, the eagerness of the cowboy cavalry troop to kill some British cavalry if war, as rumored, came—it being a matter of challenge-to-prowess among rival cavaliers. He notes the widespread racial blending of Indians and whites on the frontier and the traits of various tribes—the nobility of the Nez Perces, for example, as compared to the thieving nature of the Arapahoes.

The chapter on the bighorn sheep is a fine mix of hunting adventure, nature study and descriptive experience. The episode in which he is caught in a blizzard while meat hunting for winter fare is well described. The next day's hunt in the glittering white twenty-below-zero mountains—bagging a great ram as three bighorns floundered through the late afternoon sunlight—is vivid indeed. On this occasion TR suffered frostbite of face, foot and knees, but apparently sustained no permanent damage.

"Sheriff's Work on the Ranch" describes a prime vigilante adventure—Roosevelt and two of his men pursuing the boat thieves in a scow quickly made for the purpose, capturing them, trying to float on down the river but being stopped by the ice-jam. After eight days of grueling patrol of the three prisoners amid freezing country, with no further game available (all recently hunted out by a Sioux sweep) he finally left his men with the boats, and after thirty-six hours of sleepless march and patrol, got the prisoners into the plains hamlet of Dickinson to be put behind bars. It is a great story by a stout heart. He received fifty dollars as deputy sheriff for this 300-mile trek and the service of making the arrests. One of the two ranchers they met along the way wondered why they had not hung the varmints without all this trouble. And one of the men captured later wrote from prison inviting him to stop by for a visit if he should ever be out Bismarck way. "I have read a good many of your sketches of ranch life in the papers since I have been here, and they interested me deeply."[21] TR cites this as an example of the sense of equality and pride among the men of the West.

TR wrote *Ranch Life* partly to recoup some of the thousands he lost in this investment in western adventure. Yet he also wrote to chronicle for the future the brief primitive picture of the passing frontier.

> In its present form stock-raising on the plains is doomed, and can hardly outlast the century. The great free ranches, with their barbarous, picturesque, and curiously fascinating surroundings, mark a primitive stage of existence as surely as do the great tracts of primeval forests, and like the latter must pass away before the onward march of our people; and we who have felt the charm of the life, and have exulted in its abounding vigor and its bold, restless freedom, will not only regret its passing for our own sakes only, but must also feel real sorrow that those who come after us are not to see, as we have seen, what is perhaps the pleasantest, healthiest, and most exciting phase of American existence.[22]

Also autobiographical, *Cowboys and Kings, Three Great Letters of Theodore Roosevelt* presents editor Elting E. Morison's choices of TR's most illuminating and literary letters after he, Morison, had spent four years editing (with Joseph Blum) the *Letters of Theodore Roosevelt* in eight volumes. The letters chosen are those to John Hay, the chronicler of Lincoln and author of *Pike Country Ballads* and at the time secretary of state, August 9, 1903; to Sir George Otto Trevelyan, the elder of the two British historians named Trevelyan, October 1, 1911; and to David Gray, American novelist, October 5, 1911. All three letters were sent confidentially but with obvious expectation of later publication after all had passed on. This little volume could be *the* best place to start in getting acquainted with Theodore Roosevelt as a man of letters. They are warm, perceptive, human, but interesting as well because the president (or ex-president) was going through lively experiences while also observing them and later recording them. The first letter gives vivid glimpses of the old West, and of the swift turn-of-the-century changes that were then taking place. The second and third give perceptive analysis of the problems of kings and queens in Europe in an age of rising republics, as seen by TR during his triumphal and controversial return from Africa through Europe in 1910. It is a bit like Mark Twain in attitude and humor, without the satiric lash.

> But the ordinary king—and I speak with cordial liking of all the kings I met—has to play a part in which the dress parade is ludicrously out of proportion to the serious effort; there is a quite intolerable quantity of sack to the amount of bread.[23]

The contrasts are delightful. He shows the interest the European royalty take in the progressive democratic American "royalty" (or ex-president) who believes in doing things of the nobility (hunting, leading, fighting in wars) but who also spurns hereditary royalty and reaction and who believes all good citizens should work at something constructive (even working in a plant or selling carpets) while cultivating their minds and moral characters. On the occasion of King Edward's funeral, Roosevelt was made special ambassador from the United States to Britain. From this experience, he gives intimate glimpses of the childish bickering over protocol among the czars, emperors, kings and archdukes, humorously contrasting their antics with the attitude of an American who does "not care a rap" where he sits at the banquet or where he rides in the procession as long as it gives comfort to the British people.

He includes shrewd analysis of royal persons and nations, ever blended with his historical sense.

> Evidently the Emperor, and indeed the leaders of the North Germans generally, feel towards the English and at times even towards the French, much as the Romans of the Second Punic War felt towards Greece—a mixture

178

of overbearing pride in their own strength, and of uneasiness as to whether they really are regarded by cultivated and well-bred people as having the social position which they ought to have.[24]

This is precisely the dangerous psychological position that produced World War I and II, and bears no little resemblance to Russia's situation today. TR even suggests an effort for relieving the situation:

> I am convinced that it would make a real difference in the Emperor's feelings if occasionally some man like Londonderry, who has done something, at least titularly, in politics, and possesses great wealth and high social position, would take a house in Berlin for six weeks during the season.[25]

Such a shrewd, simple way to work for real peace.

It was on this African-European trip that TR gave forth some of his most unexpected thoughts in the form of addresses both political and cultural. In Khartoum he spoke out against the restless, rebelling Sudanese in defense of empire and civilization. In Cairo he did the same, risking assassination by what he called "Seventh Century types" of Moslems as he supported British rule as a civilizing force. In the Guildhall speech in London he forthrightly rallied the English (after clearing with the British government leaders) to support their colonial civil and military administrators in the name of Christianity and civilization. This address, with its accusations of official and public timidity, caused a storm of criticism on both sides of the Atlantic. Roosevelt also delivered a sluggish lecture called "Biological Analogies in History" at Oxford, and then, of course, had to give another, the more vigorous "Citizenship in a Republic," at the Sorbonne. This required that the Germans not be slighted; so he spoke in Berlin on "The World [Civilization] Movement." Then, of course, there was the Peace Prize to be accepted in Norway, requiring another address in Oslo. These have been published in *African and European Addresses* and several appear in *History as Literature and Other Essays.* (See bibliography.)

TR was a continuous essayist and editorialist in magazines and speeches throughout his career. As such he achieved one of his primary roles, that of moralist—as Harbaugh calls him, "the conscience of the nation."[26] Essays with titles like "American Ideals," "The Strenuous Life," "Realizable Ideals," and "Foes of our Own Household" expressed his moral philosophy and formed title works for volumes of similar productions. His basic themes were physical, mental and spiritual activity, devotion to the public good, reform of institutions and laws, the rooting out of corruption, development of individual character through self-discipline and good home life, military preparedness, cultivation of enjoyment and hope, and practical cooperation with others in society to achieve what must be done. For example, in the "Duties of American Citizenship" address to the Liberal Club in Buffalo, January 26, 1893, he said, after some opening remarks:

> The first duty of an American citizen, then, is that he shall work in politics; his second duty is that he shall do that work in a practical manner; and his third is that it shall be done in accord with the highest principles of honor and justice.[27]

Thus, though he was a tireless moralist, and worked hard to live up to his own precepts throughout his life, the political leader was never far below the surface.

He struck a popular chord—which echoes yet—in clarifying conservation as a moral issue, a balancing of public good against private greed, of long-term preservation of beauty and resources against swift, short-term destruction of even the basic economic resources then being mined out. He spoke out, in short, for everything that he or a large constituency of his culture thought good, and was enough of a wordsmith to stir millions of hearts to do better than they had been doing. He simplified politics—local, national and international—conservation, institutional reform, all kinds of subjects, by making them simple battles of good and evil. And he rallied people in a dozen fields to constructive action and results.

"The Strenuous Life," typical of the early TR philosophy, was given as a speech to the Hamilton Club in Chicago, April 10, 1899. It is studded with quotable lines: "It is hard to fail, but it is worse never to have tried to succeed.... Freedom from effort in the present merely means that there has been stored up effort in the past.... I ask only that what every self-respecting American demands from himself and from his sons shall be demanded of the American nation as a whole."[28] He gives an eloquent justification for the agony of the Civil War as fair exchange for its noble results.[29] He goes on from simply asserting the above to applying it to the nation in getting on with its duty in setting up a civilizing empire in Cuba, Puerto Rico, Hawaii, Guam and the Philippines, building up the army and navy, and getting on with being a world power (and, of course, a good and constructive one). It is a very warlike speech, justifying the Spanish American War and its military and political follow-through in U.S. foreign policy.

If we drove out a medieval tyranny only to make room for savage anarchy, we had better not have begun the task at all. It is worse than idle to say that we have no duty to perform, and can leave to their fates the islands we have conquered. Such a course would be the course of infamy. It would be followed at once by utter chaos in the wretched islands themselves. *Some stronger, manlier power would have to step in* and do the work, and we would have shown ourselves weaklings, unable to carry to successful completion the labors *that great*

181

and high-spirited nations are eager to undertake. [Italics added.][30]

In short, he is justifying the 1898 expansive surge of the United States by implying that it really was, not a subconscious surge for more territory after the closing of the frontier, but a competitive move into the Pacific power vacuum to fill it before Japan could. The whole series of 1898 episodes served notice to Japan: We see you coming up and we are coming up faster; don't get foolish ideas in regard to us. We are going to be a Pacific power (number one, thank you). This caused the Japanese surge to turn (1) against Russia (1904), (2) against Korea (1910), (3) against China (1931-37), and (4) finally, against us (1941-45).

> I preach to you, then, my countrymen, that our country calls not for the life of ease but for the life of strenuous endeavor. The twentieth century looms before us big with the fate of many nations. If we stand idly by, if we seek merely swollen, slothful ease and ignoble peace, if we shrink from the hard contests where men must win at the hazard of their lives and at the risk of all they hold dear, then the bolder and stronger peoples will pass us by, and will win for themselves the domination of the world.[31]

He did not mention Japan specifically in the speech. But he was clearly turning his championship of moral bravery and vigorous activity to the political service of American nationalism and empire in the tradition of manifest destiny.

The strong jingoism of these speeches takes them out of the realm of literature and leaves them of interest mainly as historical and biographical documents. In "Washington's Forgotten Maxim,"[32] an address before the Naval War College, June, 1897, he championed as usual military preparedness and revealed how rampant was his nationalism.

Amid some inspiring words and examples he threw in sweeping fascistic statements like this:

> We are all worse off when any of us fails at any point in his duty toward the State in time of peace, or his duty toward the State in time of war.[33]

Given beliefs like this, his strong-central-government concept, his authoritarianism and hero worship, and his belief in the necessity of controlling corporations in the national interest, it is to TR's credit that his belief in American democracy and gradual evolution toward a better life for all overpowered his strong leanings toward fascism and dictatorship. As an extremely popular president for seven and a half years he certainly had plenty of opportunities to create emergencies, wars, and crises from which he as dictator could have rescued America. But he was too much a believer in democracy to consider it.

TR apparently coined the term *muck-raker*, as applied to mud-slinging journalists, with his powerful essay, "The Man with the Muck-Rake," an address given in Washington, April 14, 1906. As always, he was rife with historical and literary allusion.

> In Bunyan's "Pilgrim's Progress" you may recall the description of the Man with the Muck-rake, the man who could look no way but downward, with the muck-rake in his hand; who was offered a celestial crown for his muck-rake, but who would neither look up nor regard the crown he was offered, but continued to rake to himself the filth of the floor.

> In "Pilgrim's Progress" the Man with the Muck-rake is set forth as the example of him whose vision is fixed on carnal instead of on spiritual things. Yet he also typifies the man who in this life consistently refuses to see aught

183

that is lofty, and fixes his eyes with solemn intentness only on that which is vile and debasing. Now, it is very necessary that we should not flinch from seeing what is vile and debasing. There is filth on the floor, and it must be scraped up with the muck-rake; and there are times and places where this service is the most needed of all the services that can be performed. But the man who never does anything else, who never thinks or speaks or writes, save of his feats with the muck-rake, speedily becomes, not a help to society, not an incitement to good, but one of the most potent forces for evil.[34]

Among the hunting and travel books should be mentioned *African Game Trails,* the result of his and son Kermit's ten-month safari from South Africa north to the Nile in 1910. It was his great postpresidential adventure, taken partly for the joy of it, and partly to clear out of the way of his hand-picked successor, Taft. Roosevelt and his party hunted the biggest and most remote game animals during the day, studied animals and collected thousands of specimens for the Smithsonian en route, while TR read rapidly from his "pig-skin library" in idle hours, and wrote punctual chapters of his book at night. If the reader can set aside the childishness of big game hunting in general, he will find this a readable and informative book. Hemingway will not fail to come to mind as the direct cultural descendant of Theodore Roosevelt.

Similarly, *Through the Brazilian Wilderness* (1914) chronicles TR's last great naturalist expedition into wild country, his last of a lifetime of feats to prove his manhood (since Wilson did not let him go to war again). What started as a trip to South America to study nature and give some lectures turned into an exploring expedition at the suggestion of the Brazilian government, and TR and Kermit got to join a brilliant Brazilian explorer, Col. Candido Rondon, to seek out the full extent of the unknown River of Doubt. After many brushes with disaster (and several lives lost), they succeeded in running this uncharted river 1500 miles to its confluence with the Amazon system, and the grateful Brazilians changed its name to Rio Roosevelt. And as always, the book is interesting, loaded with giant ferns, tapirs, anacondas and piranhas, astute observations of the people and local color, as well as a genuine chronicle of twentieth century adventure. TR almost died of a terrible fever on this trip and, as reported by Kermit, several times asked to be left behind, to relieve the others of the burden of carrying him out when supplies were almost gone. Charnwood sees this attitude, repeated by TR even in his delirium, as genuine evidence of his great character.[35]

In biography, TR's choices of subject (Thomas Hart Benton, Gouverneur Morris, Oliver Cromwell) reveal his interests—the expanding west, the American Revolution and how it achieved free government, the English Civil War and the man who first wrested public control from the monarchy. Although these subjects also reveal a love for the hero and a bent toward authoritarianism, yet there is wariness about its dangers. And further, they reveal his proper scholarly decisions to write historical and biographical works which needed to be written to fill gaps in past scholarship and knowledge. Roosevelt brought out the forgotten figure of Gouverneur Morris as a loyal and able American revolutionary, but one who was too conservative for the good of the people of the new nation. No American biographer had treated Cromwell in light of his being a predecessor of the American Revolution or a precursor of separation of church and state. TR's treatment of Cromwell shows his empathy with the virtuous authoritarian, his admiration for the skillful, innovative general, yet also his respect for the problems of achieving basic constitutional changes in that religion-torn century. Roosevelt was also inspired by John Hampden, whom he considered a brave English noble resisting an unconstitutional tax (ship money) somewhat as the colonies later resisted the Stamp Act. Yet the biographer strove to be fair, and get all the information available from all sources, and produced readable, workmanlike biographies not lacking in original insights.

Roosevelt first ventured into history with his *Naval War of 1812*, published just two years after he emerged from Harvard. In fact, he could see little point in writing papers to please professors, and more or less undertook this research to assert his own ability to write creatively and produce readable history on a worthwhile area that *he* felt needed explication and balance. Though like any military history it becomes a dreary succession of grievous battles, it is competently done, filling a need for a history examining fairly that aspect of that war. It also solidified TR's views on the stupidity of military unpreparedness and the incompetence of Jefferson and Madison in properly defending the country. It also undoubtedly helped Roosevelt qualify later for appointment as assistant secretary of the Navy (1897-8) from which position he lobbied frantically to precipitate the Spanish-American War —for the reasons already mentioned.

The Winning of the West, published in six small volumes in 1889 through 1896, four volumes in 1905, and two volumes in 1917, is TR's most ambitious work. It expressed his love for the West, his nationalism and pride in the English-speaking peoples, his love of war, valor and glory, his realism concerning the brutality of that long conquest and settlement, his seriousness as a scholar and historian, and his commitment to the writing of informative and accurate yet readable, understandable, *living* history along the lines of his admired model, Francis Parkman.[36] Any volume will teach one history and bring to life the struggles and peoples and many of the remarkable characters of this great saga. Henry F. Pringle, author of *Theodore Roosevelt: A Biography* (1931) has said, "*The Winning of the West* had the best literary quality of all his books."[37]

Less of literary than of subject matter interest are his natural history pieces, his various letter collections, and his shelf on politics and international relations. Those interested in the latter should of course see also his congressional

186

messages and state papers—yet many of this group are not without vigor and literary ability. An excellent one-volume selection from Roosevelt's political and social thought is William Harbaugh's *Writings of Theodore Roosevelt* (1967)—sixty-seven selections, many of which make stirring and incredibly modern-sounding reading indeed. Included are selections from what was essentially TR's last book, *Roosevelt in the Kansas City Star* (1921), a series of 114 editorials written for that paper, sometimes praising, often blasting Wilson's handling of the war. An example of the vigor of the young elder statesman's pen may be found in the October 26, 1918, editorial:

Those of us who believe in unconditional surrender regard Germany's behavior during the last five years as having made her the outlaw among nations. In private life sensible men and women do not negotiate with an outlaw or grow sentimental about him, or ask for a peace with him on terms of equality if he will give up his booty. Still less do they propose to make a league with him for the future, and on the strength of this league to abolish the sheriff and take the constable. On the contrary, they expect the lawofficers to take him by force and to have him tried and punished. They do not punish him out of revenge, but because all intelligent persons know punishment to be necessary in order to stop certain kinds of criminals from wrong-doing and to save the community from such wrong-doing.

We ought to treat Germany in precisely this manner. It is a sad and dreadful thing to have to face some months or a year or so of additional bloodshed, but it is a much worse thing to quit now and have the children now growing up obliged to do the job all over again, with ten times as much bloodshed and suffering, when their turn comes. The surest way to secure a peace as lasting as that which followed the downfall of Napoleon is to overthrow the Prussianized Germany of the Hohenzollerns as Napoleon was overthrown. If we enter into a league of peace with Germany and her vassal allies, we must expect them to treat the arrangement as a scrap of paper whenever it becomes to their interest to do so.[38]

Theodore Roosevelt as writer is worth reading today for a number of reasons:

1. He is an interesting writer (especially for all males), treating of seamanship, adventure, big game hunts, valor, history, local color—cowboys and czars, New York politicians and African bushmen—people, politics, wildlife, in a world struggling for order, personalities of celebrated people, and causes dear to the man on the street. He is also the male chauvinist par excellence whom female readers might wish to read to study the archetype in action, hailing motherhood, big families, fidelity, chastity and loyalty to home and no double standard. Yet he also was a champion (before there were any women voters) of women's suffrage, decent minimum wages and eight-hour days for women (rather than the ten- or twelve-hour days then common), no matter what the commercial cost to those industries employing women.

2. He writes with a vivid and frequent humor, both the humor of anecdote (the New York spoils system county-clerk making $82,000 a year from fees, while hiring his deputy to do his clerk work for $1,500)[39] and the humor of his own astounding personality and life (insisting on going on with his October 14, 1912, speech in Milwaukee after a would-be assassin shot him in the chest, the bullet having been slowed in its path by the fat speech manuscript he had tucked in his vest).[40]

3. He is a fearless, straight-talking moralist, facing up to every tough question of his day with realism, hard thinking, and strong character. He is not afraid to go behind clichés or sacred cows to the root question (Can the government control corporations? Can the people retain and protect their own

forests?) and come up with clear, fair answers without equivocation. (Yes, they can and here's how:).

4. Many of his struggles are still very much our struggles today: Controlling rampant industrialism and big corporations for the public rather than merely the private interest. Controlling our use of natural resources for the same end. How do we reform and reshape our institutions to achieve social justice (a fine TR phrase) while retaining the capitalistic engine of opportunity to better oneself and acquire a return proportional to initiative and service rendered? How do we achieve world order and the progress of civilization in a jungle of competing nationalisms? (Walk softly, carry a big stick, and work for justice and arbitration of differences among nations.) The followers of both Ralph Nader and Richard Nixon, of both Kenneth Galbraith and Huey Newton, will find much to inspire them on principle in the readable writings of Theodore Roosevelt.

5. TR has much to convey in basic attitude to the dejected scholars and cynical citizens of the present. He closed his speech to the American Historical Association, December 27, 1912, (the essay, "History as Literature") as follows:

Those who tell the Americans of the future what the Americans of today and of yesterday have done will perforce tell much that is unpleasant. This is but saying that they will describe the archetypical civilization of this age. Nevertheless, when the tale is finally told, I believe that it will show that the forces working for good in our national life outweigh the forces working for evil, and that, with many blunders and shortcomings, with much halting and turning aside from the path, we shall yet in the end prove our faith by our works, and show in our lives our belief that righteousness exalteth a nation.[41]

6. Perhaps the basic appeal of his writing is the excitement and interest of his own life. He is an excellent example from

almost our own times of the power of the creative and synthesizing individual to live joyously (despite tragedy) and to constructively make things happen in the directions he sees they ought to go. He lived and died a happy man, and for forty years moved mountains around him with the power of his spirit.

VII

Woodrow Wilson

Woodrow Wilson
Writer, Leader, Prophet

*We preserve it, perhaps, only because Burke wrote it;
and yet when we read it we feel inclined to pronounce it
worth keeping for its own sake.*[1]

> Wilson's essay on Burke,
> "Interpreter of English Liberty"

Though Woodrow Wilson was a fluent and prolific writer
(twelve solid books plus a five-volume *History of the American
People*), he was not a literary man per se. His writing is mostly
scholarly, historical, constitutional, political or governmental,
with a few great subjects of supreme importance (such as his
advocacy of the League of Nations) and a few essays of general
cultural interest. He was a competent scholar—a first-rate
textbook writer, an eloquent speaker first and last, a con-
summate politician (with a few grievous exceptions) most of
his public life, and occasionally a great statesman—but

seldom a producer of literature.

Yet upon such subjects he is a writer of exceptional verve and fluency, a decidedly literary scholar, historian, and constitutionalist; and he is without doubt one of America's most literate statesmen in terms of output, eloquence, readability, significance of subject matter, and size of vision. As a matter of fact, though he was highly successful as a state governor and domestic and war president, he failed singularly though understandably as a statesman in the worldwide arena, failing to persuade his own nation and other nations to modify their "sovereign" thinking in favor of world order. Wilson biographer Charles Seymour has said that Wilson was more significant as a prophet than as a statesman, and that we and future generations have still to live up to the magnificent possibilities of his American dream for the world.[2]

Yet Woodrow Wilson is perhaps the fitting man with whom to end this series, since he brings out so clearly the role of the writer-speaker in propelling the mere theoretician into the political arena. He, like all the others in this group, succeeded admirably in combining the man of thought with the man of action, while frankly indicating his preference for success as the latter. He clarified in his revealing personal essay, *Leaders of Men,* the difference between the literary man (perceptive to many facets of the *individual* man and desirous of exact, orderly, complete expression) and the leader (perceptive to an uncanny degree of how men *in the mass* will react and skillful in persuading them to do what he sees must be done). Wilson clearly admired the leader, i.e., the great persuader, more than the seer or the simply brilliant writer. He showed this in his second level praise of Burke[3] as a marvelous writer-parliamentarian but a failure as a leader. Yet it is an irony of history that this man, Wilson, chosen from among the most successful academics to lead the nation (and a series of nations) in the greatest war yet generated on earth, should ultimately have failed in the peacemaking as the superstatesman who was not quite persuasive enough. Thus he emerged from the ruins as indeed not the successful man of action but—what he thought to be little better than a failure—simply the greatest seer, moralist and prophet of his age.

Perhaps he would be comforted by his own words from *Leaders of Men* as they apply to his own book, *Woodrow Wilson's Case for the League of Nations:* "A book is often quite as quickening a trumpet as any made of brass and sounded in the field."[4] We can only work and pray that man will learn in time to listen to the trumpet of Woodrow Wilson and fashion in the spirit of the League some more practical instrument of world law.

A glance at Appendix D will reveal that Wilson wrote successfully in a number of traditional subject areas: government, history, historiography, philosophy, politics and international relations, and in addition a category I have used in place of biography—leadership. Yet it is obvious that Wilson's one great subject is power, its acquisition by the most capable leaders, parties, nations and its responsible exercise through good governmental design and the moral character of the people and their leaders. And a study of Wilson cannot long escape the three phases of his career, each in its way a stage in his unorthodox but highly unified pursuit of leadership.

I. PROFESSOR OF POLITICS

In one sense Wilson's writing belongs almost entirely to his preleadership period, 1879-1902, from then on his thought assuming the form of oratory, letters and state papers. Indeed, three of his last major works, *Constitutional Government in the United States, A Crossroads of Freedom,* and *Woodrow Wilson's Case for the League of Nations* were made up from edited shorthand transcriptions of series of lectures and speeches and some Wilson-written messages. Yet these nonetheless reflect his thought accurately in his own language and do form the full-length entities we call books. Yet they are the by-products of action as much as they are deliberate exercises in thought, and it would be fair to say that Wilson was an innovative, productive writing-professor until tapped for leadership at Princeton. And from that day on he never deliberately wrote another book.

His elevation to the Princeton presidency (after a brilliant career as a teaching, speaking professor who could also publish significantly) was the beginning of the fulfillment of his lifelong search for highest political leadership. He had always had a battle raging within him between the thinker-writer and the doer—with a decided bias in favor of the doer (see *Leaders of Men*). And, of course, he found that the chief executive of a large university or a state or a great nation had no time for academic exercises in thought but had to produce far more writing and thinking in his day-to-day search for results through action than did even the most diligent scholar. He discovered in short why the complete works of Washington (not known as a writer) now run to thirty-seven volumes, most of which are effective pieces of writing for the purposes at hand. And Wilson relished the difficult battles to creatively think and do in the arena of public affairs while maintaining his position as leader of the people.

Wilson's chief works from his academic period include *Congressional Government* (1885); *Division and Reunion, 1829-1889* (1893); *George Washington* (1896); *The State* (1898), a history of the evolution of government; and *A History of the American People* (1901-2), five volumes, later enlarged to ten volumes with the inclusion of many original documents. In addition, he was, like Theodore Roosevelt, a frequent and fluent essayist and public speaker, gaining continuous publication of creditable essays in academic and intellectual periodicals. His *History,* for example, ran serially for a year and a half in *Harper's Magazine* (1901-2), while simultaneously with the start of this work, *Atlantic Monthly* was publishing his essay, "The Reconstruction of the Southern States."[5] He collected a number of these essays, including

"A Calendar of Great Americans" and the one on Burke, in his 1896 volume, *Mere Literature and Other Essays*. Previous essays on Bismarck and Pitt as well as "Cabinet Government in the United States" (a plea for a parliamentary adaptation in the U.S. government) indicate his continuous interest in power and its responsible exercise.

Wilson began to establish his reputation as an original thinker while yet a senior at Princeton with his excellent article, "Cabinet Government in the United States." It was published in August, 1879, in *International Review*, then edited by—irony of history—young Henry Cabot Lodge. It is a persuasive attack on the glaring weakness of the U.S. system, that of granting almost absolute power over legislation to small bipartisan congressional committees which not only make their decisions in closed sessions and are thus beyond public control and accountability, but are not integrated in their decisions with any overall legislative program. To remedy this abandonment of democracy Wilson proposed an interesting reform: that the president be required to appoint his cabinet from within Congress, those members retaining their congressional seats while becoming the administration's leaders in each departmental field, including its legislation. This would evolve quickly, he felt, into a responsible ministry type of government in which the government secretaries would either carry their department's legislation before the whole of congress or resign and allow an opposition secretary to be appointed. Not only is the legislature then held responsible for its legislation (through open debate and recall), but

> ... a responsible Cabinet constitutes a link between the executive and legislative departments of the Government which experience declares in the clearest tones to be absolutely necessary in a well-regulated, well-proportioned body politic.[6]

He expressed here for the first time his lifelong belief in the

power of absolute publicity to enhance responsible government.

> The public [by this plan] is thus enabled to exercise a
> direct scrutiny over the workings of Executive depart-
> ments, to keep all their operations under a constant
> stream of daylight. Ministers could do nothing under
> the shadow of darkness; committees do all in the dark.[7]

Young Wilson believed we should also adopt this system for
the sizeable impetus it would give to the development of
statesmanship, the development of the conditions wherein the
wisest and best, the most able men of the nation, would be
encouraged into politics and leadership positions, by the
obvious opportunities and competitive rewards of the system.
"It is opportunity for transcendent influence, therefore, which
calls into active public life a nation's greater minds. . . ."[8]

> Certain it is that statesmanship has been steadily dying
> out in the United States since that stupendous crisis
> during which its government felt the first throbs of life.
> In the government of the United States there is no place
> found for the leadership of men of real ability. Why then
> complain that we have no leaders.[9]

Though his analysis is in one sense naive, and is now almost a
century old, it in several aspects pinpoints departures from
democracy and true efficiency of design that are glaringly
evident in American government today.

He pursued the same theme much further when, after an
unsuccessful year attempting to practice law, he returned to
scholarship at Johns Hopkins University. His doctoral dissertation, *Congressional Government,* was a brilliant and
readable analysis of our system as it operated, not as it was
designed in theory. The book was published in 1885 even
before his degree was awarded. It immediately established his

name as an authority in the field of government, and it exposed with merciless clarity the absolute sway held by the "disintegrate forty-seven standing committees" of Congress, a system which positively prevented open debate, accountability, recall, or a unified legislative program.

In skillful, smooth image-filled writing he makes the dark complexities unreel swiftly for the reader. For example, writing of the developments after the adoption of the U.S. Constitution Wilson says:

> There straightway arose two rival sects of political Phar-
> isees, each professing a more perfect conformity and
> affecting greater "ceremonial cleanliness" than the
> other. The very men who had resisted with might and
> main the adoption of the Constitution became, under
> the new division of parties, its champions, as sticklers for
> a strict, a rigid, and literal construction.[10]

The essence of his theme is that Congress runs the government (despite the check-and-balance theory—writing as he was in an era of weak presidents) and that the standing committees run Congress. They in turn are run by the handful of committee chairmen, all of whom are appointed by the speaker, the political boss of the majority party members. The number of House members and the number of committees preclude any independent action by the individual members or any intelligent consideration of important, complex bills by the whole legislature. All these committees, moreover, are working independently in special interest areas, making their major decisions outside of the open light of the House floor, deciding the policy of the country in small, private caucuses to which no member of the public is privy. The worst flaw in the whole system, according to Wilson, is the impossibility of there being any way for the public to identify who is precisely responsible for any one particular piece of legislation and hold him (them) accountable.

I know not how better to describe our form of government in a single phrase than by calling it a government by the chairmen of the Standing Committees of Congress. This disintegrate ministry, as it figures on the floor of the House of Representatives, has many peculiarities. In the first place, it is made up of the elders of the assembly; for, by custom, seniority in congressional service determines the bestowal of the principal chairmanships; in the second place, it is constituted of selfish and warring elements; for chairman fights against chairman for use of the time of the assembly, though the most part of them are inferior to the chairman of Ways and Means, and all are subordinate to the chairman of the Committee on Appropriations; in the third place, instead of being composed of the associated leaders of Congress, it consists of the dissociated heads of forty-eight "little legislatures" (to borrow Senator Hoar's apt name for the Committees); and, in the fourth place, it is instituted by appointment from Mr. Speaker, who is, by intention, the chief judicial, rather than the chief political, officer of the House.[11]

While not advocating a reform directly as he did in "Cabinet Government," in *Congressional Government* he is seeking through explication not only the understanding of the American legislative system but, by implication, its reform as well. He constantly implies, as he describes the present government operation, the need to increase the efficiency and workable democracy of our government by placing more power *and responsibility* in all its major offices. Concentrating power in the hands of congressional leaders responsible for the entire legislative function and subjecting them to totally public debate with an articulate, ambitious opposition (and instant recall)—these are the best ways to correct the oligarchical realities of Congress. Wilson wants that undemocratic secret committee government replaced by open, true

200

national democracy responsive to the people's will, party discipline, and good leadership.

He sees as one great advantage of responsible ministry government a large increase in the public's interest in, and consequent knowledge of, government. This effect would be achieved, as in the British system, through the drama of public debate and the excitement of great personalities and ministries placed in meaningful combat over who can best serve the public.

> The ordinary citizen cannot be induced to pay much heed to the details, or even to the main principles, of law making, unless something else more interesting than the law itself be involved in the pending decision of the lawmakers. If the fortunes of a party or the power of a great political leader are staked upon the final vote, he will listen with the keenest interest to all that the principal actors may have to say, and absorb much instruction in so doing. But if no such things hang in the balance, he will not turn from his business to listen; and if the true issues are not brought out in eager public contests . . . he will certainly never find them or care for them, and there is small use in printing a "Record" which he will not read.[12]

Though Wilson sticks admirably to his purpose of not proposing solutions to the conditions he illuminates so well, he does show how the British system corrects all these abuses and pins down responsibility and authority in the one standing committee, the majority of the House of Commons. The British thus gain "perfected party government"—i.e., unified, coordinated, well-debated, championed and criticized legislation by the one group responsible for the policy of the government.

No one can overestimate the immense advantage of a

facility so unlimited [as the British M.P.'s right to question the ministry] for knowing all that is going on in the places where authority lives. The conscience of every member of the representative body is at the service of the nation.[13]

More importantly, Wilson seems to be clarifying sources of oligarchic rule and democratic frustration within our highly touted "self-government" which are still very much with us today.

He is particularly convincing where he demonstrates how the British design improves the national budget-setting and taxation processes. The Commons as a whole sits first as a committee of supply (what we must spend, in each area); when the budget has been thus determined, the whole of Commons then becomes a committee of ways and means (how we shall raise that amount). The responsible majority ministry leads all the battles (and wins them too, or leaves the field in favor of a new ministry). By contrast in the U.S. Congress, "The national income is controlled by one Committee of the House and one of the Senate; the expenditures of the government are regulated by fifteen Committees of the House and five of the Senate...." (plus the currency controlled by two more House committees and one more Senate committee).[14]

The chairman of the [House Ways and Means] Committee figures as our minister of finance, but he really, of course, only represents [aside from his home district] the commission of eleven over which he presides.[15]

Despite the massive increases in government expenditures— and almost a century of congressional and presidential evolution—since 1885, we can sense that much of this multi-headedness (or more properly, headlessness) in our government is still there. Wilson puts it succinctly:

202

We have in this country, therefore, no real leadership because no man is allowed to direct the course of Congress, and there is no way of governing the country save through Congress, which is supreme.[16]

Perhaps Wilson has put his finger on the root cause for the headlong delegation by Congress of power to the presidency and executive departments which has occurred during this century; but the result is, if anything, more oligarchical and less truly representative government than before. At least we know we have not achieved Wilson's goal: clearly identified authority and flexible responsible government which is constantly improving its effectiveness of response to the needs of its citizens and the nation.

He assesses the Senate and president as well as the House and concludes that the president, by the limits of the constitution as it has evolved, will always be too weak to dominate Congress, lead the nation, and effect a coordinated policy. (Later, given the example of Theodore Roosevelt, he changed his mind and decided that the individual president could make the office as strong as he had the capacity to make it.) Yet in *Congressional Government,* Wilson outlines precisely the "flaw" in Senate power over the president in the making of treaties that thirty-five years later would frustrate him in getting the League of Nations accepted. He calls it the "treaty-marring power."[17]

In conclusion he gives a fine essay on the dilemmas of lawmaking and praise for Congress as a lawmaker (the maker of more laws than any other body on earth);[18] yet he questions its efficacy as a maker of the best laws possible at any given time and in any given situation. He suggests the possibility that "repeal was more blessed than enactment," in some cases. And he thinks other important duties—which are slighted due to the committee system—rest upon Congress. These are (1) the vigilant oversight of the administration (the executive branch), and (2) the instruction of the people on political affairs and issues through open debate, discussion, opposition, interrogation and complete accountability.[19]

> The informing function of Congress should be preferred even to its legislative function . . . [;] the only really self-governing people is that people which discusses and interrogates its administration.[20]

Another key work in understanding Wilson is his reflective essay, *Leaders of Men*, already mentioned. This forty-page address was first given at commencement at the University of Tennessee, on June 17, 1890, and elsewhere several times; but Wilson chose to withhold it from *Mere Literature* (or any other publication)—perhaps, as editor T. H. V. Motter speculates, because it revealed too much about Wilson's own inner struggle during the crucial 1885-96 decade, the struggle between the man of thought and the man of action. Motter, in his introduction to the 1952 Princeton publication, says, "The solution he formulated in the essay proved to be the solution of his problem," i.e., the executive Wilson winning out over Wilson the scholar.[21] Further references by Motter reveal Wilson's burning ambition to have some active (executive) post in government—supposedly to learn government better to be a better professor—but the fierce fire of ambition for power breaks through. In 1887 Wilson commented desperately to a friend, "Thirty-one years old and nothing done!"[22]

In the essay itself Wilson clarified his view (in opposition to that of the writer of these essays) that subtle literary men cannot be leaders and vice versa because of a different kind of sensibility. The literary man, according to Wilson, has too fastidious and sensitive a taste to put up with the crude translations of his thought into action which comprise all actual collective deeds; whereas the leader, not sensitive to many views but his own, has no trouble—in fact feels a joy—in accepting whatever crude deeds he can get to approximate achievement of his policy.[23] By this description, Woodrow Wilson stood too firm in the role of prophet in his last days to compromise in order to get us into the League in some fashion—or perhaps the people instinctively distrusted an Articles of Confederation type of nongovernment with real power.

The speech is studded with gems of analysis. Of Burke, Wilson says: "His power was literary, not forensic; he was no leader of men; he was an organizer of thought, but not of party victories."[24] He shows how the principle of simplicity of idea and sincerity of expression combine to persuade men in the speeches of John Bright and Richard Cobden of Britain.[25] Wilson had already said:

Men are not led by being told what they don't know. Persuasion is a force, but not information; and persuasion is accomplished by creeping into the confidence of those you would lead.[26]

"If you would be a leader of men, you must lead your own generation, not the next."[27] "Successful leadership is a product of sympathy, not of antagonism."[28] "Society is not a crowd, but an organism; and like every organism, it must grow as a whole or else be deformed."[29] "The dynamics of leadership lie in persuasion, and persuasion is never impatient."[30] Many of the lines vibrate with forecast of his own future success, and failure.

The ear of the leader must ring with the voices of the people. He cannot be of the school of the prophets; he must be of the number of those who studiously serve the slow-paced daily need.[31]

Perhaps Wilson's final peacemaking disaster was due to his own departure from his own best 1890 analysis of the art of leadership. In second-rating Voltaire, this brilliant American scholar who had swayed audiences but never held office was challenging himself to action:

> There are literary men, nevertheless, who fail of being leaders only for the lack of initiative in action; who have the thought, but not the executive parts of leaders; whose minds, if we may put it so, contain all the materials for leadership, but whose wills spend their force, not upon men, but upon paper.[32]

And in his finale he says: "I . . . conceive the leader [to be] the deeply human man, quick to know and to do the things that the hour and his nation need."[33]

Typical of his published essays are those collected in the 1896 volume, *Mere Literature and Other Essays.* As one might suspect, his title essay is an excellent advocacy of the importance of reading, enjoying and understanding literature in this age of science, business, industry and big government—and even in this age of linguistics, style-study, minor-author study, everything but the real appreciation of literature. Wilson asserts that understanding literature is essential to the citizen who wishes to understand people, their loves, hates, beliefs, ideals, dreams, myths, attitudes—all of which are the most essential thing for the student, the scholar, the jurist, the political aspirant to learn. "It is not knowledge that moves the world, but ideals, convictions, the opinions or fancies that have been held or followed."[34] (As usual, he is thinking about the enjoyment of life through effective action in those fascinating fields: human relations, leadership, power.)

He has harsh words for the scholasticism which has developed in the study of literature.

> . . . the scientific study of literature has likewise become a study of apparatus,—of the forms in which men utter thought, and the forces by which those forms have been

206

and still are being modified, rather than of thought itself.[35]

. . . there is no science of literature.[36]

He sees the need for a constructive imagination, i.e., a literary imagination, even in the writing of history and other nonfiction. And he discusses in vigorous language the sometimes antagonistic relationship of scholarship to literature.

Literature can do without exact scholarship, or any scholarship at all, though it may impoverish itself thereby; but scholarship cannot do without literature. It needs literature to float it, to set it current, to authenticate it to the race, to get it out of closets, and into the brains of men who stir abroad.[37]

His own vigor of writing is evident in the very words with which he champions vigor of writing.

The scholar finds his immortality in the form he gives to his work. It is a hard saying, but the truth of it is inexorable: be an artist or prepare for oblivion.[38]

Also in the *Mere Literature* volume appear highly readable tributes to Walter Bagehot ("A Literary Politician") and Edmund Burke ("Interpreter of English Liberty"). Within both, Wilson continually analyzes the relationship between the intellectual and the political leader, finding between them a special, admirable breed (like himself), the political intellectual who can not only analyze public affairs clearly, but can reach people with his writing art: "The literary politician, let it be definitely said, is a very fine, a very superior species of the man thoughtful."[39] His sketch of Bagehot presents the ideal: a man of wit, prescience, and literary talent who can write on business, politics, government or literature with equal perception.

> Occasionally, a man is born into the world whose mission it evidently is to clarify the thought of his generation, and to vivify it; to give it speed where it is slow, vision where it is blind, balance where it is out of poise, saving humor where it is dry,—and such a man was Walter Bagehot.[40]

He also characterizes Bagehot as "the man who first clearly distinguished the facts of the English Constitution from its theory,"[41] the very role Wilson aimed for in post-Civil War America.

In "Interpreter of English Liberty" Wilson presents a lively fifty-page sketch of Burke along with high praise: " . . . the authentic voice of the best political thought of the English race. . . . There is no page of abstract reasoning to be found in Burke. . . . he perceived that questions of government are moral questions."[42] He shows Burke's great vision and literary talent with eloquent passages from his speeches and books, passages which reflect the best spirit of the man. Wilson's last twenty pages give a most emphatic and inspiring picture of Burke the man, the progressive yet moderate political leader, the inspiring orator, the voice of England.

Wilson's histories from his academic period, *A History of the American People* (1902) and *The State* (1898), are outstanding textbooks for their day, providing that day with cores for excellent studies of the subjects presented. Yet as massive, complete textbooks, they are of little literary interest.

In *George Washington* (1896) Wilson displays his skill as a historian and writer while simultaneously revealing his obsession with leadership and foreshadowing remarkable parallels with his own future role. His sketch of Washington's trials in the two years after Yorktown, holding the collapsing confederation together by the sheer force of his personality, is not unparallel to Wilson's later, though less successful, struggle at Versailles. Within a decidedly sympathetic biography, Wilson writes lively, readable, accurate history with few quotations and no footnotes, summarizing swiftly from his generally identified sources. Yet the selection of George Washington as subject, and the notice given his executive ability shown even when he was a boy, hint that Wilson is as interested in what it takes to be a leader as he is in George Washington the man. Yet George Washington the man soon begins to emerge as a complex pillar of character, one with initiative, drive, attention to detail and a sense of follow through—one who was fated to rise to greatness. Wilson also clarifies the emergent young officer of the French and Indian War as a fighter who loved this combat for its excitement and its importance. (Who will get the continent? Who can build a great new nation?) We find tremors of this same combative-constructive spirit in all the strong presidents of our history: the Adamses, Jefferson, Jackson, Polk, Lincoln, both Roosevelts and, of course, Wilson himself.

Wilson's subsidiary sketches of Patrick Henry, Samuel Adams and John Adams show his skill as a literary historian and his continuous interest in political leadership. For example, of Samuel Adams, he says:

He was in Philadelphia now wearing the plain suit and spending the modest purse with which his friends and partisans had fitted him out—the very impersonation of the revolution men were beginning so to fear. No man had ever daunted him; neither could any corrupt him. He was possessed with the instinct of agitation: led the people, not the leaders; cared not for place, but only for power; showed a mastery of means, a self-containment, a capacity for timely and telling speech, that marked him a statesman, though he loved the rough ways of a people's government, and preferred the fierce democracy of the town meeting to the sober dignity of senates. Like an eagle in his high building and strength of audacious flight, but in instinct and habit a bird of the storm. Not over-nice what he did, not too scrupulous what he devised, he was yet not selfish, loved the principles he had given his life to, and spent himself without limit to see them triumph.[43]

Wilson illustrates in *George Washington* again his excellent sense of how not to write too much. For example, his chapter entitled "General Washington" chronicles Washington's seven years of war in a swift thirty pages. Wilson's statement about Washington, "he was a man of action rather than of parliaments," expresses not only Wilson's judgment as an historian but his ideal of leadership and successful living as well. He is frequent in his reminders of the active life Washington led, surveying, riding, hunting, being the gracious host or honored guest—as well as administering public and private business. And Wilson is fascinated by how Washington learned to be a good executive on his two great estates, handling all the correspondence of a complex business at home and in London, judging men, leading men, and giving everyone constructive jobs to do and seeing that they did them. "His estates gave him scope of command and a life of action."[44]

George Washington is an easy to read, accurate, yet informative book, one aimed at the public, not at the historian. If scholar Arthur Link finds the scholarship weak and the interpretation flimsy,[45] perhaps he does not sense that Wilson is doing two other things: teaching himself what he wants to know about Washington as a leader, and running for president of the United States by tying himself to the earlier great Virginian and American. If Wilson writes with a conservative Virginian (and a patriotic American) bias for his subject, perhaps it is because no one can study George Washington without being filled with admiration and respect.

II. REFORMER IN ACTION

"Literary men can say strong things of their age," observes Mr. Bagehot, *"for no one expects that they will go out and act on them."*[46]

Woodrow Wilson
"A Literary Politician"

The astounding thing about Woodrow Wilson was that he was able to say strong things about his age and then effectively act upon them. He was able to make the leap from being simply the astute professor of politics to being a remarkably successful political leader. One is tempted to assume that the candidate had been grooming himself all along—especially after reading in Wilson's early letter to his sweetheart, "my heart's *first* primary ambition and purpose was . . . for . . . a statesman's career."[47] In an earlier letter he wrote: "The profession I chose was politics; the profession I entered was the law."[48] Even his scholarship all seems to be pointed, as he admitted of his *History of the American People,* toward the instruction of *himself* rather than the instruction of others.[49] His astonishing executive career, for which he had been preparing all his life, began in 1902 when he was elevated to the presidency of Princeton as the climax of his remarkable years as professor. After a mixed, though substantial, success there, he was ousted over a graduate school battle just in time to be tapped in 1910 to run for governor of New Jersey— picked by the political bosses as a clean but harmless conservative front for their own continued control of the state. Much to their chagrin, the harmless professor turned progressive crusader between nomination and election and insisted not only on running his own administration but on ridding the state of political and corporate corruption, according to his promises. Wilson's success here, riding the tide of progressivism started by Roosevelt, caused him to be tapped in turn as Democratic candidate for the presidency in 1912. And there the Taft-Roosevelt split enabled the eloquent Democrat to win, becoming the eighth Virginian to enter the White House.

Not even Theodore Roosevelt had accomplished so meteoric a rise. Scarcely in United States history had a man been elected president with less political experience. And almost unheard of was the case of a state (then the nation) granting its highest office to a college president and a scholar. Surely the devout Calvinist Woodrow Wilson could be pardoned for assuming that he had been raised up by the Lord to lead the nation.

His reforms in New Jersey included a direct primary law, a corrupt practices act, an employers' liability act, establishment of a public utilities commission, legislation enabling commission form of government for cities, and a series of acts to protect the public from exploitation by trusts. As president he carried through the 1913-14 wave of reforms which included the lowering of tariffs, the graduated income tax, currency and banking reform (the Federal Reserve Act), and the regulation of trusts (the Federal Trade Commission Act and the Clayton Antitrust Act). The latter act also removed labor unions from antitrust legislation thus legalizing strikes and collective bargaining. From then on his problems with foreign policy (Mexico, the Caribbean, neutrality in the face of the World War) clouded and finally obscured the brilliant successes of his early administrations; and then the second term called forth less happy but perhaps greater achievements as a successful war president.

His writing during his executive phase turned from scholarship and political practice to educational theory and administration, campaign speeches, legislative programs and state papers. He continued to be called on constantly as a speaker and was greatest (as he had been as a professor) when speaking extemporaneously to large audiences whom he was able to grip, sway and inspire while delivering highly literary bodies of thought.

One excellent, unified book, assembled from shorthand recording of a lecture series, was *Constitutional Government in the United States* (1908). It is his final, mature essay on the actual operation of the living American constitution, bringing forward in time and understanding the earlier treatment he had made in *Congressional Government*. It is a truly literary explanation of this great subject, flowing forth with clarity, image and example, teaching from a wealth of knowledge with verve and fire: "A constitutional government is one whose powers have been adapted to the interests of its people and to the maintenance of individual liberty."[50] "Political liberty is the right of those who are governed to adjust government to their own needs."[51] "There is no such thing as corporate liberty. Liberty belongs to the individual or it does not exist."[52] "The reality of constitutional government resides in its courts."[53] No wonder he had consistently packed a 300-seat lecture hall at Princeton.

After the momentous and successful 1912 campaign, William Bayard Hale assembled a small volume comprised of about one-fourth of Wilson's campaign speeches, as well as a few prior speeches not identified as such; these were published in 1913 under the title (Wilson's campaign phrase), *The New Freedom*. A later editor, John Wells Davidson, complains that this book, though helpful in giving the main aspects of Wilson's development as a candidate, is tantalizingly incomplete since it deals with the speeches as written rather than as actually delivered, omits most of the speeches, and gives no satisfactory documentation as to the time, place and circumstances of presentation. It also conveys little of Wilson's spontaneous genius to speak on the spot without notes (as he did in all these speeches except the nomination acceptance speech at Sea Girt, New Jersey), and thus build his articulation of the New Freedom platform while in direct touch with the people. To remedy these defects, Davidson, working with Charles Swem's original shorthand notes of what Wilson actually said, has brought out a much more complete volume, *A Crossroads of Freedom* (1956).[54] This volume is important in showing how the thinking necessary for campaign speeches helped develop the candidate's own policies and program and how Wilson grew in stature and authority during this truly crossroads campaign. It also shows how Wilson again moved left (i.e., toward the center) between nomination and election and grew from being merely a successful reform governor in a single state to a truly national reform leader during this campaign.

Of course, both Wilson and Roosevelt favored reforms to control the powerful corporations of the times. Yet Wilson's "New Freedom" (under the guidance of Louis Brandeis) sought to control trusts by "regulation of competition," adjustments by government to make the economy run without special privilege, whereas Roosevelt's "New Nationalism" sought more outright "regulation of monopoly," along direct trustbusting lines. Perhaps the distinction is more rhetorical than real; but the author's general impression is that Roosevelt's new nationalism was more paternalistic and socialistic than Wilson's, since Roosevelt had been thinking about the national-industrial-judicial power relationships in real terms far longer than had Wilson. Yet ironically, aided by the Republican-Bull Moose split, Wilson was rapidly appropriating TR's positions (a process he continued to carry on throughout his first term) while riding the psychologically higher wave of being a fresh, clean, citizen candidate from outside the corrupt establishment.

Wilson's statements of ideals, goals and plans are remarkable on two counts: (1) how much of the program promised he was able to actually carry out, and (2) how many of his statements of purpose or ideals made before he came to power seemed to fit his own case when looked at from this side of his later life. His goals for government are also interesting for the way they are perennially there to be achieved anew as generation after reform generation passes away.

These works by Woodrow Wilson are worth reading today

for the insight they give into his powerful mind and personality, and for the literary verve of his expression on many occasions. They introduce to the reader a recent living example of the possibility of a man doing in high places what he says ought to be done. He is an example of the importance of self-dedication, thought, hard analysis, and artistry of expression in making things happen as they ought to happen.

III. PROPHET OF WORLD ORDER

Wilson in his last role may be represented by three or four samples of his voluminous writing as war president. First, "The Fourteen Points" speech to Congress, given on January 8, 1918, outlines his generous peace aims to induce the Germans and Allies to negotiate a peace. The first five points (open covenants, freedom of the seas, free trade, international arms control, arbitration of colonial disputes) reflect Wilson's belief that America must fulfill her destiny (as Lincoln foresaw), that of leading all men to freedom. Yet Wilson adds to that dream the audacity of starting *here and now* to do it, aiming to end the stupendous carnage and stupidity of world war, using America's moral and economic power to plunge ahead boldly (Point Fourteen) into world organization, a confederation of many nations for peace, free trade, and, by implication, worldwide freedom and democracy (control of governments by their people). It is a series of great ideas that we still must implement, or we will destroy many more millions—and perhaps all life on this planet. These ideas were ahead of their time perhaps, but only due to human stupidity, selfishness, fear, parochialism and ignorance. Wilson boldly assumed the world leader role, not for selfish or nationalist reasons, but to make real use of the opportunity of this agonizing war to create a new system among nations: to achieve and encourage worldwide public control of the awful engines of nationalism, militarism and technology.

215

An evident principle runs through the whole program I have outlined. It is the principle of justice to all peoples and nationalities, and their right to live on equal terms of liberty and safety with one another, whether they be strong or weak. Unless this principle be made its foundation no part of the structure of international justice can stand. . . . The moral climax of this the culminating and final war for human liberty has come.[55]

Second, Wilson's speech at Mount Vernon on July 4, 1918, entitled "The Four Supplementary Points," is a praiseworthy attempt at a latter-day Gettysburg Address.[56] It is a brief effective expression of Wilson's concept of America's role (and Wilson's own) in the World War and in history.

From these gentle slopes they [George Washington and the other leaders of the Revolution] looked out upon the world and saw it whole, saw it with the light of the future upon it, saw it with modern eyes that turned away from a past which men of liberated spirit could no longer endure. It is for that reason that we cannot feel, even here, in the immediate presence of this sacred tomb, that this is a place of death. It was a place of achievement. A great promise that was meant for all mankind was here given plan and reality.[57]

His principles are beautiful in their idealism—though perhaps self-satirizing as an impossible program to achieve. They include these ideas: no national right to make war; clear right of each people to decide, presumably by vote and representative assembly, vital issues concerning it; and the acceptance of a world rule of law among nations. Yet Point Four (compulsory arbitration of international disputes through a permanent World Court) is eminently practical if agreed to by all or even most powerful nations.

These great objects can be put into a single sentence: What we seek is the reign of law, based upon the consent of the governed and sustained by the organized opinion of mankind.[58]

Who could seek a higher goal, or write a purer expression of it?

Third, Wilson's "Address to the Third Plenary Session of the Peace Conference," given on February 14, 1919,[59] is another significant sample from Wilson's final period. This speech is basically a presentation to the conference of the completed Covenant of the League of Nations as tentatively adopted by fourteen nations. It was to Wilson if not to the rest of the world, "the world, expressing its conscience in law."[60] It was also "the combined Governments of the world."[61] It was "in one sense a belated document. . . . the conscience of the world has long been prepared to express itself in some such way."[62] We are for "the [complete] publicity of all international agreements."[63] "We are done with annexations of helpless people."[64] "There is very great significance, therefore, in the fact that the result was reached unanimously."[65] (The nations who thought they were agreeing with the United States on a worldwide fire brigade against future wars were Britain, France, Italy, Japan, Belgium, Brazil, China, Greece, Czechoslovakia, Poland, Portugal, Rumania and Serbia. Even the list mocks the concept of "nation" by listing Serbia and China, Greece and the United States side by side as equals. And a unanimous approval was almost meaningless without Germany, Russia, a free India and a number of others also joining in.)

Yet the efforts, the magnificent efforts of Wilson, are no less than toward the formulation of an Articles of Confederation for the World—in the grand hope, of course, of going on to a World Constitution, "the reign of law, based upon the consent of the governed and sustained by the organized opinion of mankind." Not for nought had he studied government all his life, written a biography of Washington and a history of the American people. He had been preparing and running for the presidency of the United States all his life; and now he was running hard—on the harrowing minefields of achievement—to be the first president of the world—or at least the Thomas Jefferson of world union.

He failed, of course, due to his failures as a political leader at home (after an awesome war and seven years in office) and the unripeness of the United States of America for such a great step forward. Yet to have gone ninety percent of that incredible way was a series of feats of high statesmanship, and Woodrow Wilson should be revered not only as one of the great seers of all time, but as one of the great doers, who had practical faith that high ideals of honesty, justice and equality could be—must be—the basis of practical, workable, efficient arrangements among men. His failure, though due in part to several of his own shortcomings, is America's and the world's failure as well; and Wilson's tragedy is the great Greek drama of modern times. With Wilson's fall have come subsequent failures of accord over which millions upon millions have since been slain.

William Bayard Hale, the same prominent newspaperman who edited Wilson's 1913 book of speeches, *The New Freedom*, saw Wilson's basic failure to be one of literary style. While the president was campaigning for the adoption of the League of Nations in 1918 and 1919, Hale wrote a slim volume of criticism, *The Story of a Style*. In it he demonstrated his view that a prominent reason for this gigantic failure was Wilson's failure to influence the American people. He traces this weakness specifically to a lack of strong verbs and an overdependence on adjectives, comparing Wilson unfavorably in this respect to Carlyle, Macaulay, Stevenson, Poe, Shakespeare, Scott, Dickens, Hardy, Shaw, Twain, Stendhal, and Maeterlinck.[66] Few writers would fare well when so compared, but Hale's analysis is interesting, for he emphasizes the possible close relationship between the powerful writer and the effective political leader.

Perhaps Wilson's last error lay in not getting himself assassinated by a fanatic Kaiser or Lodge supporter before the final votes on the Versailles Treaty and the acceptance of the League were taken. With his knowledge of American history, it is almost surprising that he did not arrange it. He was certainly willing to die for the sound establishment of the League. Yet because of his Virginia heritage, perhaps he felt he just might succeed in doing the impossible, as Jefferson, Washington, Madison and Monroe had done before him.

The basic weaknesses of the League were as follows: (1) the defeated nations (especially Germany and Russia) did not join it until much later—and then soon parted company; (2) it was a confederation, not a federation, and the world was far from ready for world federation; and (3) the United States did not join it (by six votes in the Senate) and soon repudiated Wilson (as the British later would repudiate Churchill), leaving the enforcement of the Versailles Treaty hanging in limbo. Yet only partially can these failures be attributed to Wilson. They are as much the failures of vision, discipline, and follow-through in the American people (led by isolationists like Lodge and Harding) as they are the failures of Wilson. As he said in one of his last calls for the ratification of the treaty-league package:

> The conception of the great creators of the [American] Government was absolutely opposite to this. They thought of America as the light of the world as created to lead the world in the assertion of the rights of peoples and the rights of free nations; as destined to set a responsible example to all the world of what free Government is and can do for the maintenance of right standards, both national and international.

> This light the opponents of the League would quench.

They would relegate the United States to a subordinate role in the affairs of the world.

Why should we be afraid of responsibilities which we are qualified to sustain and which the whole of our history has constituted a promise to the world we would sustain! This is the most momentous issue that has ever been presented to the people of the United States, and I do not doubt that the hope of the whole world will be verified by an absolute assertion by the voters of the country of the determination of the United States to live up to all the great expectations which they created by entering the war and enabling the other great nations of the world to bring it to a victorious conclusion, to the confusion of Prussianism and everything that arises out of Prussianism. Surely we shall not fail to keep the promise sealed in the death and sacrifice of our incomparable soldiers, sailors and marines who await our verdict beneath the sod of France.[67]

His great goal still stands before us, gleaming through the tarnish of his shattered hopes. The United Nations, accepted to a far greater degree than the League, still staggers between oblivion and glory under the unanimity-rule millstone. Yet all major nations are now members, and the concepts of limitation of the sovereign rights of nations and the powers of governments over peoples—and the consciousness of the need for world law—have broadened considerably. Every thinking man in every industrialized society senses the need for the control of warfare as the most dangerous of man's many potentials for self-destruction—a control which obviously requires some sort of world unity, arbitration of differences, and a fairer distribution of wealth. Yet still in the age of nations, the missiles poise in silos and submarines, the biological weapons wait in warehouses, and armed satellites float silent above the spinning earth. Will the United States, will the human race, meet the incredible challenge?

Woodrow Wilson had a soaring faith that, yes, of course, with God's ceaseless help, we would.

APPENDICES

Appendix A

Recommended Lincoln Readings as Literature

"The Perpetuation of Our Political Institutions" (also called "Speech to the Young Men's Lyceum"), January 27, 1838.

"Letter from the Lost Townships" (a satirical short story), August 27, 1842.

"A Parable of the Kansas-Nebraska Law,"* from a Lincoln-written editorial in the Illinois *Journal,* plus two paragraphs from the famous Peoria speech on the same subject, October 16, 1854.*

Last half of the "Dred Scott Decision Speech," Springfield, June 26, 1857.

"A House Divided: Speech to the Republican State Convention," June 16, 1858.

Fragment of the Speech at Edwardsville, Illinois, September 11, 1858.

"Cooper Institute Address," New York, February 27, 1860.

"Farewell at Springfield," February 11, 1861.*

"Independence Hall Remarks," February 22, 1861.

"First Inaugural Address," March 4, 1861.

Last two paragraphs from the Message to Congress, December 1, 1862.

The Gettysburg Address, November 19, 1863.

A few of his more literary letters and fragments: to Mrs. Bixby, General Joseph Hooker, James C. Conkling, Horace Greeley; "On Slavery"; "Meditation on the Divine Will."*

"Response to a Serenade," November 10, 1864.

"Second Inaugural Address," March 4, 1865.

"Last Public Address," April 11, 1865.

* Items quoted in full within chapter five.

223

Most, if not all, of these works are to be found in all general collections of Lincoln's writings. See Roy P. Basler, ed., *Abraham Lincoln: His Speeches and Writings* New York (1946); or Roy P. Basler, Marion Dolores Pratt, and Lloyd A. Dunlap, eds., *The Collected Works of Abraham Lincoln,* 9 vols., New Brunswick, N. J. (1953-55).

Appendix B

Address delivered by Abraham Lincoln at the dedication of the Cemetery at Gettysburg, November 19, 1863.

Four score and seven years ago our fathers brought forth on this continent, a new nation, conceived in Liberty, and dedicated to the proposition that all men are created equal.

Now we are engaged in a great civil war, testing whether that nation, or any nation so conceived and so dedicated, can long endure. We are met on a great battle-field of that war. We have come to dedicate a portion of that field, as a final resting place for those who here gave their lives that that nation might live. It is altogether fitting and proper that we should do this.

But, in a larger sense, we can not dedicate—we can not consecrate—we can not hallow—this ground. The brave men, living and dead, who struggled here, have consecrated it, far above our poor power to add or detract. The world will little note, nor long remember what we say here, but it can never forget what they did here. It is for us the living, rather, to be dedicated here to the unfinished work which they who fought here have thus far so nobly advanced. It is rather for us to be here dedicated to the great task remaining before us—that from these honored dead we take increased devotion to that cause for which they gave the last full measure of devotion—that we here highly resolve that these dead shall not have died in vain—that this nation, under God, shall have a new birth of freedom—and that government of the people, by the people, for the people, shall not perish from the earth.

Appendix C

Theodore Roosevelt's Major Works

Autobiographical:
  Autobiography, 1913.
  Diaries of Boyhood and Youth, 1928.
  The Rough Riders, 1899.
  Ranch Life and the Hunting Trail, 1888.

Essay:
  American Ideals, 1897.
  The Strenuous Life, 1901.
  African and European Addresses, 1910.
  Realizable Ideals (the Earl Lectures), 1912.
  History as Literature and Other Essays, 1913.
  Fear God and Take Your Own Part, 1916.
  Book-Lover's Holiday in the Open, 1916.
  Foes of Our Own Household, 1917.
  Great Adventure, 1918.

Hunting and Travel:
  The Wilderness Hunter, 1893.
  Hunting Trips of a Ranchman, 1885.
  Outdoor Pastimes of an American Hunter, 1905.
  African Game Trails, 1910.
  Through the Brazilian Wilderness, 1914.

Biography:
  Thomas Hart Benton, 1886.
  Gouverneur Morris, 1899.
  Oliver Cromwell, 1900.

History:
  The Naval War of 1812, 1882 (First book at age 24).
  The Winning of the West, 6 vols., 1886-89.
  New York, 1891.
  Hero Tales from American History (with Henry Cabot Lodge),
    1895.

Natural History:

Theodore Roosevelt's America: Selections from the Writings of the Oyster Bay Naturalist, ed. Farida A. Wiley, 1955.

Life Histories of African Game Animals (with Edmund Heller), 1914.

"Dear and Antelope of North America," his share of T. S. Van Dyke, D. G. Elliot, A. J. Stone and Theodore Roosevelt, *The Deer Family,* 1902.

Selected Letters:

Cowboys and Kings: Three Great Letters of Theodore Roosevelt, ed. Elting E. Morison, 1954.

Theodore Roosevelt and His Time Shown in His Own Letters, ed. J. B. Bishop, 1919.

Theodore Roosevelt's Letters to His Children, ed. J. B. Bishop, 2 vols., 1920.

Letters to Anna Roosevelt Cowles, 1924.

Selections from Correspondence of Theodore Roosevelt and Henry Cabot Lodge, 1925.

Politics, National and International:

The New Nationalism, 1910.

Progressive Principles, 1913.

America and the World War, 1915.

Roosevelt in the Kansas City Star, 1921.

Selections from throughout his works:

Writings of Theodore Roosevelt (selections from his political and social thought), ed. William H. Harbaugh, 1967.

Theodore Roosevelt Cyclopedia, ed. A. B. Hart and H. R. Ferleger, 1941.

Theodore Roosevelt Treasury: A Self-Portrait from his Writings, ed. Hermann Hagedorn, 1957.

Theodore Roosevelt: Free Citizen (selections from his writings and stories from his record), Hermann Hagedorn, 1956.

Basic Collections: (The last on this list would generally include the foregoing.)

"Messages and Papers of Theodore Roosevelt," *A Compilation of Messages and Papers of the Presidents, 1789-1909*, ed. James D. Richardson, rev. ed., 11 vols., 1909.

Theodore Roosevelt: Presidential Addresses and State Papers, 8 vols., 1910.

Letters of Theodore Roosevelt, ed. Elting E. Morison and Joseph Blum, 8 vols., 1951-54.

Public Papers of Theodore Roosevelt, Governor, 2 vols., 1899-1900.

Works of Theodore Roosevelt, ed. Hermann Hagedorn, 24 vols., 1925.

Appendix D

Woodrow Wilson's Principal Writings

Government:
Cabinet Government in the United States, 1879.
Congressional Government: A Study in American Politics, 1885.
Constitutional Government in the United States, 1908.
The State (a history of the evolution of government), 1898.
"Character of Democracy in the United States," *Atlantic Monthly*, LXIV (November 1889), 577-88.
"The English Constitution," *Chautauquan*, XII (October 1890-January 1891), 5-9, 149-54, 293-98, and 430-34.
"The Government and Business," *Princeton Alumni Weekly*, VIII (November 27, 1907), 160-62.
"Leaderless Government," Address, Virginia Bar Association, August 4, 1897.
"Responsible Government under the Constitution," *Atlantic Monthly*, CVII (April 1886), 542-53.
History:
A History of the American People, 5 vols., 1902. 10 vols., as enlarged with original documents, 1918.
Division and Reunion, 1829-1889, 1905.
"The Course of American History," *Mere Literature*, 1896.
"The Significance of American History," preface to *Harper's*

Encyclopedia of United States History, 10 vols., 1905, I, xxi-xxvi.

Historiography and Authorship:
"Mere Literature," "The Author Himself," "The Truth of the Matter," and "A Literary Politician" (on Walter Bagehot), *Mere Literature,* 1896.

International Relations:
International Ideals, 1919.
Woodrow Wilson's Case for the League of Nations, compiled with his approval by Hamilton Foley, 1923.

Leadership:
Leaders of Men (an 1890 address and essay), 1952.
"Leaderless Government," Address, Virginia Bar Association, August 4, 1897.
"Interpreter of English Liberty" (on Edmund Burke), *Mere Literature,* 1896.
George Washington, 1896.
"The Study of Administration," *Political Science Quarterly,* II (June 1887), 197-222.
"The Spirit of Jefferson," *Princeton Alumni Weekly,* VI (April 28, 1906), 551-54.

Politics:
The New Freedom, 1913.
A Crossroads of Freedom, the 1912 Campaign Speeches, 1956.
An Old Master and other Political Essays, 1893.
"Conservatism, True and False," *Princeton Alumni Weekly,* IX (December 16, 1908), 186-89.

Philosophy:
"Ideals of Public Life," *Princeton Alumni Weekly,* VIII (November 27, 1907), 160-62.
On Being Human, 1919.

Letters and Collected Writings:
The Priceless Gift: The Love Letters of Woodrow Wilson and

Ellen Axson Wilson, ed. Eleanor Wilson McAdoo, 1962. (Perhaps the most forthright, personal and revealing of all his writing, also showing the large influence his wife had upon his entire rise to greatness.)

Public Papers of Woodrow Wilson, ed. Ray S. Baker and William E. Dodd, 6 vols., 1925-27.

Ray S. Baker, *Woodrow Wilson: Life and Letters* (an authorized biography with extensive quotation of his letters), 8 vols., 1927-39.

NOTES

Introduction

1. Woodrow Wilson. *Mere Literature and Other Essays,* (1965), 20, 26.

2. Quoted from Walter Bagehot in Woodrow Wilson, "A Literary Politician," *Mere Literature,* 86.

3. Woodrow Wilson, *Leaders of Men,* ed. T. H. V. Motter (1952), 15.

4. S. E. Morison, *Oxford History of the American People* (1965), 829.

5. Benjamin Franklin, *Autobiography,* ed. Max Farrand (1949), 80-81.

6. John Adams, Letter to Timothy Pickering, August 6, 1822, *The Works of John Adams,* ed. Charles F. Adams, 10 vols. (1850-56), II, 514n.

7. Theodore Roosevelt, *Autobiography,* ed. Wayne Andrews (1958), 222.

8. Abraham Lincoln, "Independence Hall Remarks," February 22, 1861, as quoted in T. Harry Williams, ed., *Abraham Lincoln: Selected Speeches, Messages, and Letters* (1957), 137.

Chapter One

1. Cited in Benjamin Franklin, *Papers of Benjamin Franklin, 1706-1790,* ed. Leonard W. Labaree, William B. Willcox, and others, 20 vols. (1959-72) (hereafter referred to as *Papers*), X, 81-82.

2. Richard Amacher, ed., *Franklin's Wit and Folly: The Bagatelles* (1953), 25.

3. John Adams, *The Works of John Adams,* ed. Charles F. Adams, 10 vols. (1850-56), I, 663-64.

4. Benjamin Franklin, *Autobiography,* ed. Max Farrand (1949), 18-19.

5. *Autobiography*, 23-25.

6. Henry W. Spiegel, *The Rise of American Economic Thought* (1960), 9.

7. *Autobiography*, 81.

8. Benjamin Franklin, *Writings of Benjamin Franklin*, ed. Albert H. Smyth, 10 vols. (1905-7) (hereafter referred to as *Writings*), IV, 4.

9. *Autobiography*, 116-17.

10. Nathan G. Goodman, ed., *A Benjamin Franklin Reader* (1945), 39.

11. Perry Miller, ed., *Major Writers of America* (1966), 5.

12. Benjamin Franklin, *Poor Richard's Almanac* (selections), ed. Paul L. Ford (no date), 8, 17, 19, 21, 22, 27, 31.

13. Miller, 8. See also Robert Newcomb, "The Sources of Franklin's Sayings of Poor Richard," an unpublished dissertation, University of Maryland, 1957. See also Richard E. Amacher, *Benjamin Franklin*, 61-66.

14. Richard E. Amacher, *Benjamin Franklin* (1962), 28-31. Principal studies referred to here are, besides Newcomb's above, Lois M. MacLurin, *Franklin's Vocabulary*, 1928, and Francis X. Davy, "Benjamin Franklin, Satirist: The Satire of Franklin and Its Rhetoric," an unpublished dissertation, Columbia University, 1958. Amacher calls the latter "the most penetrating and complete work yet accomplished on Franklin's satire," 183.

15. William W. Clary, *Benjamin Franklin, Printer and Publisher* (1935), 34.

16. *Writings*, VI, 127-37; first printed in the *Public Advertiser*, September 11 and 22, 1773.

17. *Public Advertiser, Writings*, VI, 131-37.

18. Verner W. Crane, "Three Fables of Franklin," *New England Quarterly*, IX (September 1936), 499. See also by the same author *Benjamin Franklin's Letters to the Press, 1958-77* (1950).

19. Miller, 36.

20. Carl Van Doren, *Benjamin Franklin* (1938), 774.

21. *Writings*, X, 86-91; essay dated March 23, 1790, and printed in the *Federal Gazette*.

22. Lewis J. Carey, *Franklin's Economic Views* (1928), 72-73.

23. *Writings*, IV, 231.

24. Carey, 57.

25. *Writings*, IV, 231.

26. *Writings,* IV, 49.

27. Goodman, 376; essay first published as a pamphlet, 1749.

28. Letter to Sir Joseph Banks, Passy, July 27, 1783; reprinted in Goodman, 659-60.

29. Goodman, 25.

30. Amacher, *Franklin's Wit and Folly,* 54.

31. Amacher, *Franklin's Wit and Folly,* 91-92.

32. Goodman, 462.

33. Goodman, 497.

34. Goodman, 517-21.

35. Carl Van Doren, *Franklin's Autobiographical Writings* (1945), 694.

36. *Papers,* X, 81-82.

Chapter Two

1. Gilbert Chinard, *Honest John Adams* (1964), 23.

2. John Adams, *The Works of John Adams,* ed. Charles F. Adams, 10 vols. (1850-56) (hereafter referred to as *Works*), II, 100.

3. *Works,* I, 23.

4. John Adams and James and Mercy Warren, *The Warren-Adams Letters,* 2 vols. (1925), I, 201-2.

5. *Works,* IX, 418-20.

6. *The Warren-Adams Letters,* I, 321-22.

7. John and Abigail Adams, *Familiar Letters of John Adams and His Wife Abigail Adams* (1876), 381.

8. *Works,* IX, 546.

9. *Works,* VIII, 369-70.

10. Adrienne Koch and William Peden, eds., *Selected Writings of John and John Quincy Adams* (1946) (hereafter referred to as *Koch*), 70.

11. *Works,* VIII, 300.

12. *Works,* II, 9.

13. *Works,* II, 17-18.

14. *Works,* II, 107.

15. John Adams, *Diary and Autobiography of John Adams,* ed. L. H. Butterfield and others, 4 vols. (1961), I, 337.

16. *Works,* II, 323-24.

17. *Works,* II, 338.

18. *Works,* III, 448-64; passage cited on 462.

19. *Works,* III, 466-67.

20. Catherine Drinker Bowen, *John Adams and the American Revolution* (1949), 511-12.

21. Chinard, 78-79.

22. *Works,* IV, 37-38.

23. Koch, 50.

24. *Works,* II, 514.

25. *Works,* IV, 288-89.

26. *Works,* IV, 444-45.

27. Koch, 125.

28. *Works,* VI, 234-35.

29. Edwin H. Cady, ed., *Literature of the Early Republic* (1950), 117-18.

30. Koch, 167.

31. *Works,* X, 67-68.

32. *Works,* X, 283-84.

33. *Works,* X, 415.

34. *Works,* X, 416.

Chapter Three

1. John Adams, *The Works of John Adams,* ed. Charles F. Adams, 10 vols. (1850-56), II, 514.

2. Adrienne Koch and William Peden, eds., *Life and Selected Writings of Thomas Jefferson* (1944) (hereafter referred to as Koch), 350.

3. Koch, 290.

4. Gilbert Chinard, *Honest John Adams* (1964), 334.

5. Abraham Lincoln, Letter to Henry L. Pierce and others, April 6, 1859, in T. Harry Williams, ed., *Abraham Lincoln: Selected Speeches, Messages, and Letters* (1957), 113.

6. John Locke, *Second Treatise on Government,* in J. M. Smith and Paul Murphy, eds., *Liberty and Justice,* 2 vols. (1958), I, 13-15.

7. Koch, 298.

8. Koch, 299.

9. Koch, 294.

10. Gilbert Chinard, *Thomas Jefferson, Apostle of Americanism*, rev. ed. (1939), 48.

11. Koch, 297-98.

12. Koch, 303.

13. Koch, 309.

14. Koch, 307.

15. Koch, 309.

16. Koch, 309.

17. Koch, 310.

18. Koch, 310.

19. Koch, 311.

20. Saul K. Padover, *Thomas Jefferson and the Foundations of American Freedom* (1965) (hereafter referred to as *Foundations*), 40.

21. Carl Becker, "The Literary Qualities of the Declaration," *The Declaration of Independence* (1945), 222.

22. Koch, 22-28.

23. Koch, 25.

24. Becker, 212-17. In the same place Becker finds Lincoln much the greater writer than Jefferson: "This something, which Jefferson lacked but which Lincoln possessed in full measure, may perhaps for want of a better term be called a profoundly emotional apprehension of experience." Perhaps this difference can be detected in the next three quotations.

25. Text of the original draft of the Declaration as given in Jefferson's *Autobiography*, with the changes made by Congress not distinguished; Koch, 22.

26. Williams, 114.

27. Koch, 109-10.

28. Chinard, *Thomas Jefferson*, 115-18.

29. Chinard, *Thomas Jefferson*, 119.

30. Koch, 201-6.

31. Koch, 202.

32. Koch, 221-27.

33. C. W. Ceram, "Mr. Jefferson's Dig," *American History Illustrated*, VI (November 1971), 38-41.

34. Koch, 236ff.

35. Koch, 278.

36. *Foundations*, 92.

37. *Foundations*, 92.

38. Koch, 51.

39. Koch, 263.

40. Koch, 265.

41. Koch, 262.

42. Koch, 265.

43. Koch, 265.

44. Koch, 265.

45. To Colonel Charles Yancey, 1816, in Saul Padover, *Thomas Jefferson on Democracy* (1939) (hereafter referred to as *On Democracy*), 149.

46. Koch, 269.

47. Koch, 269.

48. Koch, 275.

49. Koch, 276.

50. Koch, 276-77.

51. Koch, 280.

52. Koch, 285.

53. Koch, 285.

54. Koch, 2.

55. Koch, 60-61.

56. Henry Steele Commager, "Jefferson, Thomas," *The World Book Encyclopedia* (1960), X, 60.

57. Koch, 84-85.

58. Koch, 104.

59. Koch, 108-9.

60. Koch, 107.

61. Koch, 96-97.

62. Koch, 116.

63. Koch, 126-27.

64. Koch, 145-46.

65. Koch, 158.

66. Koch, 158.

67. Koch, 323.

68. Koch, xl.

69. Koch, xl.

70. Commager, 65.

71. To Madison, 1789, *On Democracy,* 159.

72. To Destutt de Tracy, *On Democracy,* 159.

73. To Washington, 1788, *On Democracy,* 156.

74. To LaFayette, 1820, *On Democracy,* 155.

75. To Kosciusko, 1810, *On Democracy,* 154.

76. To Samuel Kercheval, 1816, *On Democracy,* 155.

77. Koch, frontispiece.

Chapter Four

1. Henry Steele Commager, "John Quincy Adams," *The World Book Encyclopedia* (1960), I, 34.

2. John Quincy Adams, *The Writings of John Quincy Adams,* ed. W. C. Ford, 7 vols. (1913-17) (hereafter referred to as *Writings*), I, 65-73.

3. Adrienne Koch and William Peden, eds., *Selected Writings of John and John Quincy Adams* (1946) (hereafter referred to as Koch), 323.

4. *Writings*, VI, 61-62.

5. John Quincy Adams, *Diary of John Quincy Adams, 1794-1848,* ed. Allan Nevins (1969) (hereafter referred to as *Diary*), xiii.

6. The other American Ghent negotiators were Albert Gallatin, Henry Clay, and James A. Bayard.

7. Walter Lafeber, ed., *John Quincy Adams and American Continental Empire* (1965), 13.

8. *Writings,* VII, 316.

9. Charles Beard and Mary Beard, *New Basic History of the United States* (1944), 238.

10. Lafeber, 24-25.

11. John Quincy Adams, *Memoirs of John Quincy Adams,* ed. Charles F. Adams, 12 vols. (1874-77) (hereafter referred to as *Memoirs*), IV, 502-3.

12. Josiah Quincy, *Memoir of the Life of John Quincy Adams* (1858), 384.

13. *Memoirs,* V, 12.

14. Lafeber, 13.

15. Lafeber, 13-14.

16. *Diary,* 573.

17. Mary Cable, *Black Odyssey* (1971), 1-99. See also *The Amistad*

Case: Africans Taken in the Amistad (U.S. 26th Cong., 1st Sess., H. Exec. Doc. 185) (New York, 1840). This document, containing all the government papers relating to this case, was published due to a resolution of Congress introduced by John Quincy Adams. It has been reprinted, together with Adams's argument before the Supreme Court (published separately in 1841), by the Basic Afro-American Reprint Library (New York, 1968).

18. *Writings,* VII, 191-92.
19. *Writings,* III, 340-41.
20. *Writings,* IV, 128.
21. *Writings,* IV, 209.
22. *Writings,* VII, 468-69.
23. *Memoirs,* XI, 441.
24. *Diary,* xxvii.
25. Quincy, 382-83.
26. *Diary,* 474-75.
27. John Quincy Adams, *Parties in the United States* (1941), 7-8.
28. Koch, 329.
29. *Diary,* 503.
30. *Diary,* 509.
31. *Diary,* 489.
32. *Diary,* 39.
33. *Diary,* 508-9.
34. *Diary,* 413.
35. *Diary,* 511.
36. Cable, 65.
37. *Diary,* 465.
38. *Diary,* 489.
39. *Diary,* 483.
40. *Diary,* 485.
41. *Diary,* 24.
42. *Diary,* 487.
43. *Diary,* 490.
44. *Diary,* 468.
45. *Diary,* 468-69.
46. *Writings,* IV, 406-9.
47. *Diary,* 519.

Chapter Five

1. Don E. Fehrenbacher, *Abraham Lincoln: A Documentary Portrait through His Speeches and Writings* (1964), xxv.

2. Roy P. Basler, "Lincoln's Development as a Writer," Introduction to Roy P. Basler's one-volume edition of selections, *Abraham Lincoln: His Speeches and Writings* (1969), 12.

3. Allan Nevins, "Lincoln in His Writings," Introduction to Philip Van Doren Stern, *Life and Writings of Abraham Lincoln* (1940), xvii.

4. Basler, 193.

5. Basler, 148-56.

6. Basler, 152.

7. Basler, 12.

8. Jacques Barzun, *Lincoln, the Literary Genius* (1960), 11-12.

9. Barzun, 17.

10. Barzun, 18.

11. T. Harry Williams, ed., *Abraham Lincoln: Selected Speeches, Messages, and Letters* (1957), 268.

12. Basler, 568.

13. Basler, 708-9.

14. Basler, 335-36.

15. Barzun, 29.

16. Barzun, 38.

17. Carl Sandburg, *Abraham Lincoln: The Prairie Years and the War Years,* one-volume edition (1954), 571-72.

18. Letter to Andrew Johnston, Basler, 184.

19. Fehrenbacher, xxvii.

20. Williams, 34.

21. Basler, 655.

22. Basler, 8.

23. Basler, 9.

24. Basler, 537.

25. Basler, 538-39.

26. Basler, 567-68.

27. Williams, 39-40.

28. "The 14th Section," an editorial in the Illinois *Journal,* September 11, 1854, Basler, 281-82.

29. Basler, 314-15.

30. "Annual Message to Congress," December 1, 1862, Basler, 679.

31. Williams, 190-91.

32. Basler, 688.

33. Williams, 198.

34. Basler, 81.

35. Basler, 81.

36. Basler, 83.

37. Williams, 5.

38. Basler, 85.

39. Basler, 84.

40. Basler, 310.

41. Basler, 283-90.

42. Elwell Crissey, *Lincoln's Lost Speech: The Pivot of His Career* (1967).

43. Crissey, 231.

44. Harry E. Pratt, Illinois State Historian, as cited in Crissey, 245.

45. Basler, 352-66. The portion recommended for literary quality is the last half, 360-66.

46. Basler, 372 (italics of original omitted).

47. Basler, 533.

48. Basler, 533-34.

49. Basler, 535.

50. Crissey, 180, 196.

51. Basler, 585.

52. Basler, 588.

53. Basler, 47-48.

54. Sandburg, 447.

55. Barzun, 16-19.

56. Jean-Francois Revel, *Without Marx or Jesus* (1971). See also Charles Reich, *The Greening of America* (1970).

57. Letter to Henry L. Pierce and others, Williams, 114.

58. Basler, 44.

59. Sandburg, 445.

60. Williams, 283.

61. Williams, 137.

62. Basler, 513 (italics of original omitted).

Chapter Six

1. Hermann Hagedorn, "Roosevelt, Theodore," *Encyclopedia Britanica* (1956), XIX, 539. Hagedorn had previously edited *Works of Theodore Roosevelt* in 24 volumes.

2. Theodore Roosevelt, *Autobiography*, Centennial edition, ed. Wayne Andrews (1958), 309.

3. William Harbaugh, ed., [Selected] *Writings of Theodore Roosevelt* (1967), xviii.

4. Harbaugh, xliv.

5. *Autobiography*, 130.

6. *Autobiography*, 138-41. Yet the episode was not without its rewards. On debarking from the ship at Montauk Point, Long Island, he was recruited to run for governor of New York on the Republican ticket (*Autobiography*, 146-49).

7. "The Recall of Judicial Decisions," Harbaugh, 267-80; episode referred to, 274.

8. Theodore Roosevelt, Letter to George Otto Trevelyan, October 11, 1911, *Cowboys and Kings: Three Great Letters of Theodore Roosevelt*, ed. Elting E. Morison (1954), 86-87.

9. Hagedorn, 541.

10. Lord Charnwood (Godfrey Rathbone Benson), *Theodore Roosevelt* (1923), 204-5.

11. *Autobiography*, 261-62.

12. Theodore Roosevelt, *The Winning of the West*, 6 vols. (1906), I, 20.

13. Harbaugh, 395.

14. *The Winning of the West*, I, 45-46.

15. The same year the *Autobiography* was published, 1913, Theodore Roosevelt also published *Progressive Principles* (his party's program in detail), and *History as Literature and Other Essays*, a collection of essays and addresses of the kind he was continually grinding out for magazine publication or special occasions. Several of the latter were speeches given before various distinguished bodies in Europe and America during the previous three years.

16. *Autobiography*, 354.

17. *Autobiography*, 222.

18. *Autobiography*, 36.

19. *Autobiography*, 108.

20. *Autobiography,* 257-58.

21. Theodore Roosevelt, *Ranch Life and the Hunting Trail* (1966), 129.

22. *Ranch Life,* 24.

23. *Cowboys and Kings,* 53.

24. *Cowboys and Kings,* 91.

25. *Cowboys and Kings,* 91.

26. Harbaugh, 248.

27. Theodore Roosevelt, *American Ideals* (1897), 283.

28. Theodore Roosevelt, *The Strenuous Life* (1901), 1-3.

29. *The Strenuous Life,* 4-5.

30. *The Strenuous Life,* 9.

31. *The Strenuous Life,* 20.

32. *American Ideals,* 182. "To be prepared for war is the most effectual means to promote peace."

33. *American Ideals,* 198.

34. Harbaugh, 294.

35. Charnwood, 181-82.

36. His essay "History as Literature," given as an address to the American Historical Association, waxes eloquent on this theme.

37. Henry F. Pringle, "Roosevelt, Theodore," *The World Book Encyclopedia* (1960), XV, 426.

38. Harbaugh, 391-92.

39. Harbaugh, 245.

40. Harbaugh, 333-44. To quiet well-wishers seeking to get him medical aid, TR said, "Don't you pity me. I am all right. I am all right and you cannot escape listening to the speech either," 336.

41. *History As Literature,* 35-36.

Chapter Seven

1. Woodrow Wilson, *Mere Literature and Other Essays,* (1896, reprinted 1965), 104-60. Wilson is referring here to Burke's early volume, *Inquiry into the Origin of Our Ideas of the Sublime and Beautiful,* 120.

2. Charles Seymour, *Woodrow Wilson and the World War* (1921).

3. Woodrow Wilson, *Leaders of Men,* a forty-page essay given first as a commencement address, University of Tennessee, Knox-

ville, June 17, 1890. Published in book form, ed. T. H. V. Motter (1952). Item referred to, 26-27.

4. *Leaders of Men*, 19.

5. Henry Jones Ford, *Woodrow Wilson, The Man and His Work* (1916), 76.

6. Woodrow Wilson, *Cabinet Government in the United States*, ed. Thomas Finletter (1947), 17.

7. *Cabinet Government*, 18.

8. *Cabinet Government*, 18.

9. *Cabinet Government*, 22-23.

10. Woodrow Wilson, *Congressional Government* (1956), 26.

11. *Congressional Government*, 82.

12. *Congressional Government*, 82-83.

13. *Congressional Government*, 197.

14. *Congressional Government*, 103.

15. *Congressional Government*, 112.

16. *Congressional Government*, 142.

17. *Congressional Government*, 52.

18. *Congressional Government*, 195.

19. *Congressional Government*, 195.

20. *Congressional Government*, 198.

21. *Leaders of Men*, 3-4.

22. *Leaders of Men*, 6.

23. *Leaders of Men*, 21-22.

24. *Leaders of Men*, 28.

25. *Leaders of Men*, 31-35.

26. *Leaders of Men*, 29.

27. *Leaders of Men*, 29.

28. *Leaders of Men*, 53.

29. *Leaders of Men*, 41.

30. *Leaders of Men*, 55.

31. *Leaders of Men*, 41.

32. *Leaders of Men*, 54-55.

33. *Leaders of Men*, 60.

34. *Mere Literature*, 10.

35. *Mere Literature*, 13.

36. *Mere Literature*, 26.

37. *Mere Literature*, 18-19.

38. *Mere Literature*, 22.

39. *Mere Literature,* 101-2.

40. *Mere Literature,* 75.

41. *Mere Literature,* 74.

42. *Mere Literature,* 105, 128, 141.

43. Woodrow Wilson, *George Washington* (1963), 156.

44. *George Washington,* 44.

45. Arthur S. Link, as quoted in John A. Garraty, *Woodrow Wilson* (1970), 24.

46. *Mere Literature,* 72.

47. Letter to Ellen Louise Axson (later Mrs. Wilson), February 24, 1885. Quoted at length in E. David Cronon, ed., *Political Thought of Woodrow Wilson* (1965), 9.

48. Letter to Ellen Louise Axson, October 30, 1883, Cronon, 4.

49. Garraty, 24-25.

50. Woodrow Wilson, *Constitutional Government in the United States* (1921), 2.

51. *Constitutional Government,* 4.

52. *Constitutional Government,* 16.

53. *Constitutional Government,* 18.

54. Woodrow Wilson, *A Crossroads of Freedom: The 1912 Campaign Speeches of Woodrow Wilson,* ed. John Wells Davidson (1956), 4-5.

55. Cronon, 445.

56. Cronon, 446-50.

57. Cronon, 446.

58. Cronon, 449.

59. Woodrow Wilson, *Public Papers of Woodrow Wilson,* ed. Ray S. Baker and William E. Dodd, 6 vols., (1925-27) (hereafter referred to as *Public Papers),* V, 413-29.

60. *Public Papers,* V, 428.

61. *Public Papers,* V, 427.

62. *Public Papers,* V, 428.

63. *Public Papers,* V, 427.

64. *Public Papers,* V, 427.

65. *Public Papers,* V, 424.

66. William Bayard Hale, *The Story of a Style* (1920), as cited in Robert Gunning, *Technique of Clear Writing* (1968), 109.

67. "Appeal to the Country," October 3, 1920, *Public Papers,* VI, 503-5.

BIBLIOGRAPHY

Introduction

Adams, John. *The Works of John Adams.* Edited by Charles F. Adams. 10 vols. Boston, 1850-56.

Franklin, Benjamin. *Autobiography.* Edited by Max Farrand. Berkeley, Calif., 1949.

Morison, S. E. *Oxford History of the American People.* New York, 1965.

Roosevelt, Theodore. *Autobiography.* 1913. Centennial edition edited by Wayne Andrews. New York, 1958.

Williams, T. Harry, ed. *Abraham Lincoln: Selected Speeches, Messages, and Letters.* New York, 1957.

Wilson, Woodrow. *Mere Literature and Other Essays.* Port Washington, N. Y., 1965.

—————. *Leaders of Men.* Edited by T. H. V. Motter. Princeton, N.J., 1952.

Chapter One

Adams, John. *The Works of John Adams.* Edited by Charles F. Adams. 10 vols. Vol. I. Boston, 1850-56.

Amacher, Richard E. *Benjamin Franklin.* New York, 1962.

—————. *Franklin's Wit and Folly: The Bagatelles.* New Brunswick, N.J., 1953.

Carey, Lewis J. *Franklin's Economic Views.* Garden City, N.Y., 1928.

Clary, William W. *Benjamin Franklin, Printer and Publisher.* Los Angeles, 1935.

Crane, Verner W., ed. *Benjamin Franklin's Letters to the Press, 1758-1775.* Chapel Hill, N.C., 1950.

—————. "Three Fables of Franklin." *New England Quarterly* IX (September 1936): 499-504.

Franklin, Benjamin. *Autobiography*. Edited by Max Farrand. Berkeley, Calif., 1949.

————. *Papers of Benjamin Franklin, 1706-1790*. Edited by Leonard W. Labaree, William B. Willcox, and others. 20 vols. New Haven, Conn., 1959-72.

————. *Poor Richard's Almanac* (selections). Edited by Paul L. Ford. Mount Vernon, N.Y., no date.

————. *Writings of Benjamin Franklin*. Edited by Albert H. Smyth. 10 vols. New York, 1905-07.

Goodman, Nathan G., ed. *A Benjamin Franklin Reader*. New York, 1945.

Ketcham, Ralph L. *Benjamin Franklin*. New York, 1966.

Miller, Perry. *Major Writers of America*. New York, 1966.

Spiegel, Henry W. *The Rise of American Economic Thought*. Philadelphia, 1960.

Van Doren, Carl. *Benjamin Franklin*. New York, 1938.

————. *Franklin's Autobiographical Writings*. New York, 1945.

Chapter Two

Adams, John. *Diary and Autobiography of John Adams*. Edited by L. H. Butterfield and others. 4 vols. Cambridge, Mass., 1961. Reprinted, New York, 1964.

————. *The Works of John Adams*. Edited by Charles F. Adams. 10 vols. Boston, 1850-56.

Adams, John, and Abigail Adams. *Familiar Letters of John Adams and His Wife, Abigail Adams*. Edited by Charles F. Adams. Boston, 1876.

Adams, John, and James and Mercy Warren. *The Warren-Adams Letters*. 2 vols. Boston, 1925.

Bowen, Catherine Drinker. *John Adams and the American Revolution*. Boston, 1950.

Cady, Edwin H., ed. *Literature of the Early Republic*. New York, 1950.

Cappon, Lester J., ed. *Adams-Jefferson Letters: The Complete Correspondence between Thomas Jefferson and Abigail and John Adams*. 2 vols. Chapel Hill, N.C., 1959.

Chinard, Gilbert. *Honest John Adams*. Boston, 1964.

Koch, Adrienne, and William Peden, eds. *Selected Writings of John and John Quincy Adams.* New York, 1946.

Smith, Page. *John Adams.* 2 vols. Garden City, N.Y., 1963.

Chapter Three

Adams, John. *The Works of John Adams.* Edited by Charles F. Adams. 10 vols. Boston, 1850-56.

Becker, Carl. *The Declaration of Independence.* New York, 1945.

Boyd, Julian P., and others, eds. *Papers of Thomas Jefferson.* 19 vols. Princeton, N. J., 1950-74.

Cappon, Lester J., ed. *Adams-Jefferson Letters: The Complete Correspondence between Thomas Jefferson and Abigail and John Adams.* 2 vols. Chapel Hill, N.C., 1959.

Ceram, C. W. "Mr. Jefferson's Dig." *American History Illustrated* VI (November 1971): 38-41.

Chinard, Gilbert. *Honest John Adams.* Boston, 1964.

—————. *Thomas Jefferson, Apostle of Americanism*, rev. ed. Boston, 1939.

Commager, Henry Steele. "Jefferson, Thomas." *The World Book Encyclopedia.* Vol. IX. Chicago, 1960.

Koch, Adrienne, and William Peden, eds. *Life and Selected Writings of Thomas Jefferson.* New York, 1944.

Lee, Gordon, ed. *Crusade against Ignorance: Thomas Jefferson on Education.* New York, 1967.

Padover, Saul K. *Thomas Jefferson and the Foundations of American Freedom.* Princeton, N.J., 1965.

—————. *Thomas Jefferson on Democracy.* New York, 1939.

Smith, J. M., and Paul Murphy, eds. *Liberty and Justice.* 2 vols. New York, 1958.

Williams, T. Harry, ed. *Abraham Lincoln: Selected Speeches, Messages, and Letters.* New York, 1957.

Wilstach, Paul. *Correspondence of Adams and Jefferson, 1812-1826.* New York, 1966.

Chapter Four

Adams, John Quincy. *Diary of John Quincy Adams, 1794-1848.*

Edited by Allan Nevins. New York, 1969.

—————. *Memoirs of John Quincy Adams*. Edited by Charles F. Adams. 12 vols. Philadelphia, 1874-77.

—————. *Parties in the United States*. New York, 1941.

—————. *The Writings of John Quincy Adams*. Edited by W. C. Ford. 7 vols. New York, 1913-17.

Amistad Case: Africans Taken in the Amistad. U.S. 26th Cong., 1st Sess., H. Exec. Doc. 185. New York, 1840. Reprinted, New York, by Basic Afro-American Reprint Library, 1968.

Beard, Charles, and Mary Beard. *New Basic History of the United States*. Garden City, N.Y., 1944.

Cable, Mary. *Black Odyssey*. New York, 1971.

Commager, Henry Steele. "Adams, John Quincy." *The World Book Encyclopedia*. Vol. I. Chicago, 1960.

Koch, Adrienne, and William Peden, eds. *Selected Writings of John and John Quincy Adams*. New York, 1946.

Lafeber, Walter, ed. *John Quincy Adams and American Continental Empire*. Chicago, 1965.

Quincy, Josiah. *Memoir of the Life of John Quincy Adams*. Boston, 1858.

Chapter Five

Basler, Roy P., ed. *Abraham Lincoln: His Speeches and Writings*. New York, 1946. Reprint. New York, 1969.

Barzun, Jacques. *Lincoln, the Literary Genius*. Evanston, Ill., 1960.

Crissey, Elwell. *Lincoln's Lost Speech: The Pivot of His Career*. New York, 1967.

Fehrenbacher, Don E., ed. *Abraham Lincoln: A Documentary Portrait through His Speeches and Writings*. New York, 1964.

Herndon, William H., and Jesse W. Weik. *Herndon's Life of Lincoln*. New York, 1889, 1930. Reprint. Cleveland, 1949.

Sandburg, Carl. *Abraham Lincoln: The Prairie Years and the War Years*. One-volume edition. New York, 1954.

Stern, Philip Van Doren. *Life and Writings of Abraham Lincoln*. New York, 1940.

Williams, T. Harry, ed. *Abraham Lincoln: Selected Speeches, Messages, and Letters*. New York, 1957.

Chapter Six

Bailey, Thomas A. *Theodore Roosevelt and the Japanese-American Crisis.* Stanford, Calif., 1934.

Charnwood, Lord (Godfrey Rathbone Benson). *Theodore Roosevelt.* Boston, 1923.

Cutright, Paul Russell. *Theodore Roosevelt the Naturalist.* New York, 1956.

Hagedorn, Hermann. "Roosevelt, Theodore." *Encyclopedia Britannica.* Vol. XIX. Chicago, 1956.

Harbaugh, William H. *The Life and Times of Theodore Roosevelt.* Rev. ed. New York, 1963.

————. *Writings of Theodore Roosevelt.* Indianapolis, 1967.

O'Gara, Gordon C. *Theodore Roosevelt and the Rise of the Modern Navy.* Princeton, N.J., 1943.

Pringle, Henry F. *Theodore Roosevelt: A Biography.* Rev. ed. New York, 1956.

————. "Roosevelt, Theodore," *The World Book Encyclopedia.* Vol. XV. Chicago, 1960.

Wagenknecht, Edward. *The Seven Worlds of Theodore Roosevelt.* New York, 1958.

Roosevelt, Theodore. *African and European Addresses.* New York, 1910.

————. *American Ideals.* New York, 1897.

————. *Autobiography.* 1913. Centennial edition edited by Wayne Andrews. New York, 1958.

————. *Cowboys and Kings: Three Great Letters of Theodore Roosevelt.* Edited by Elting E. Morison. Cambridge, Mass., 1954.

————. *History as Literature.* 1913. Port Washington, N.Y., 1967.

————. *Ranch Life and the Hunting Trail.* 1888. Reprint, Ann Arbor, Mich., 1966.

————. *The Strenuous Life.* New York, 1901. New York.

————. *The Winning of the West.* 6 vols. 1889-96. New York, 1906.

Chapter Seven

Baker, Ray S. *Woodrow Wilson: Life and Letters.* 8 vols. New York, 1927-39.

Bell, Herbert C. F. *Woodrow Wilson and the People*. Garden City, N.Y., 1945.

Blum, John M. *Woodrow Wilson and the Politics of Morality*. Boston, 1956.

Cronon, E. David, ed. *Political Thought of Woodrow Wilson*. Indianapolis, 1965.

Foley, Hamilton, ed. *Woodrow Wilson's Case for the League of Nations*. His own words compiled with his approval, 1923. Port Washington, N.Y., 1967.

Ford, Henry Jones. *Woodrow Wilson, The Man and His Work*. New York, 1916.

Garraty, John A. *Woodrow Wilson*. New York, 1970.

Hale, William Bayard. *Story of a Style*. New York, 1920.

Link, Arthur S. *Wilson*. 5 vols. Princeton, N.J., 1947, 1956, 1960, 1964, 1965.

McAdoo, Eleanor Wilson, ed. *The Priceless Gift, the Love Letters of Woodrow Wilson and Ellen Axson Wilson*. New York, 1962.

Seymour, Charles. *Woodrow Wilson and the World War*. New Haven, Conn., 1921.

Wilson, Woodrow. *A Crossroads of Freedom: The 1912 Campaign Speeches of Woodrow Wilson*. Edited by John Wells Davidson. New Haven, Conn., 1956.

—————. *Cabinet Government in the United States*. Edited by Thomas Finletter. Stamford, Conn., 1947.

—————. *Congressional Government*. New York, 1956.

—————. *Constitutional Government in the United States*. New York, 1921.

—————. *George Washington*. New York, 1963.

—————. *Leaders of Men*. Edited by T. H. V. Motter. Princeton, N.J., 1952.

—————. *Mere Literature and Other Essays*. New York, 1896. Reprint, Port Washington, N. Y., 1965.

—————. *The New Freedom*. Edited by William Bayard Hale. Garden City, N.Y., 1913.

—————. *Public Papers of Woodrow Wilson*. Edited by Ray S. Baker and William E. Dodd. 6 vols. New York, 1925-27.

249